3000 800053 73416
St. Louis Community College

Florissant Valley Library
St. Louis Community College
3400 Pershall Road
Ferguson, MO 63135-1499
314-595-4514

WITHDRAWN

St. Louis Community College

Forest Park
Florissant Valley
Meramec

Instructional Resources
St. Louis, Missouri

Front Yard America

Front Yard America:
The Evolution and Meanings of a Vernacular Domestic Landscape

Fred E.H. Schroeder

Bowling Green State University Popular Press
Bowling Green, OH 43403

Material Culture Series
General Editors
Sue Bridwell Beckham
Fred E.H. Schroeder

Copyright © 1993 by Bowling Green State University Popular Press

Library of Congress Catalogue Card No: 93-73035

ISBN: 0-87972-635-0 Clothbound
      0-87972-636-9 Paperback

Cover design by Laura Darnell-Dumm/Dumm Art

Cover photograph courtesy of the Toledo-Lucas County Public Library

Once more, for Jan and Erich;
and now for Margie and Karl too.

ACKNOWLEDGEMENTS

My interest in American front yards dates back to 1969 when I began to photograph homemade yard ornaments. My chief motive was amusement but I also began to wonder when and why these very public displays came upon the American landscape. My answers were published in 1977 as a chapter on "The Democratic Yard and Garden" in *Outlaw Aesthetics*. Ten years later as a participant in the Meanings of the Garden conference at the University of California, Davis, my interest was rekindled, but now my curiosity pierced through the idiosyncrasies of ornamentation to the underlying national design. As I explain in the first chapters of this book, researching pervasive ordinariness on a national scale is replete with problems. My research, consequently, has been serendipitous, but greatly aided by help from a variety of libraries and archives. The Libraries of the University of Minnesota and the public libraries of Duluth, Minneapolis and St. Paul have been my mainstays. The Toledo-Lucas County Library provided absolutely essential personal help as did the Minnesota Historical Society. Other important sources have been the Indianapolis Public Library, the Indiana State Historical Library, the Illinois State Historical Library, the Sangamon Valley Collection of the Springfield Public Library, the New York Public Library, the libraries of the Winterthur Museum, the Edison Institute, the Smithsonian Institution, and the Curt Teich Postcard Archives of Lake County Museum in Illinois. In England I consulted materials at the University of Birmingham and the British Library. *History News Dispatch* kindly published a request for historic photographs, and I was gratified to receive help from the Litchfield Historical Society and the Grout Museum of History and Science.

Front Yard America

My methods and conclusions are entirely my responsibility, but I must tender thanks for ideas that grew out of conversations with Jay Anderson, D. Keith Crotz, Michael Pollan and Erich Schroeder. I have also gained insights from presentations at the Popular Culture Association, the Meanings of the Garden Conference, the Winterthur Conference and especially the Association for Living History Farms and Agricultural Museums.

The manuscript has evolved by fits and starts over the past four years; Jan Stanaway of the University of Minnesota, Duluth, Department of Philosophy has with unflagging good humor processed my handscript into typescript, Barbara Nelson did the penultimate proofing, and Nancy Korby did the final processing of the manuscript. Ken Moran printed most of the illustrations; any shortcomings are due to my myopic eye and handheld cameras. Jan Schroeder has been with me looking with critical eye at yards and gardens on two continents, and laboring by my side in our yard.

A word about documentation: page numbers enclosed in parentheses in the text refer to the Works Cited. In most cases I have been able to allude to the author or title in the narrative. The small superscript numbers refer to the Notes offering more detailed explanations or critical comments.

CONTENTS

Introduction	1
Part One	
The Philistine Effect and Other Challenges in Researching Vernacular Culture	3
Part Two	
Learning About Front Yards from the Critics	17
Part Three	
Living in Front Yards and Back Yards	31
Part Four	
The Coming of the Lawn Mower	41
Part Five	
Developing an Aesthetic for the Democratic Front Yard	75
Part Six	
To Practice as I Preach: Auburndale and Scottwood	97
Part Seven	
As Toledo Goes, So Goes the Nation	103
Part Eight	
Myths and Anxieties	121
Part Nine	
Front Yard Futures: *Plus ça change, plus c'est la même chose*	137
Notes	155
Works Cited	161

INTRODUCTION

The typical American front yard is too easily defined: in cities and towns, neighboring yards of single-family homes are interconnected by a contiguous grass lawn; in rural areas where neighbors' yards are separated by fields, pastures or woods, the clipped front lawn presents an open face to passersby. It's so simple, so obvious, that it hardly seems worth comment.

Although this vernacular landscape design is not unique to the United States—the typical Canadian yard is identical and Australian landscapes are similar—it is sharply different from Old World *residential environs*; we cannot apply the term "front yard" to them even for purposes of comparison.[1] The American front yard is truly vernacular in several senses of the word. Etymologically, *vernacular* means "born in one's house," specifically a "home-born slave." J.B. Jackson, the geographer who was first to promote the study of everyday landscapes, has perceptively used American black slave quarters as a starting point in defining vernacular environments (9-13),[2] but let's set aside the slave aspect and point to the fact that the front yard is indeed a homegrown product, an indigenous invention. Unlike professional landscape architectural styles, the American front yard is not an imitation, adaptation or continuation of foreign vernacular antecedents. Of course, the term *vernacular* has been largely applied to language, but this provides some useful insights for defining vernacular landscapes. Vernacular speech is not formal, literary, educated, cultivated; but neither is it necessarily unconscious, undesigned, unadorned and inartistic. The life and liveliness of vernacular speech is to be found in dialects, which are local variants on the general vernacular. Paradoxically, most people are unaware that everyone speaks in a dialect, only becoming conscious of their own vernacular

2 Front Yard America

dialects when they have been long separated from a home locale to return to a shock of self-recognition. This is true also about our American vernacular landscape. We recognize it by contrast, not by familiarity.

Clearly then, the front yard is indeed *too* easily defined. There are not only "dialect variations" on the common patterns, but there are infinite personal variations within each dialect of the vernacular. However, my subject here is the historical evolution of the *general type* of American front yard, that is, the domestic landscape design that makes a place recognizably "American." The thesis of this essay will emerge gradually, so let me anticipate. The essence of the front yard is the unfenced lawn that serves as a public ornament. As a positive aesthetic, it developed in Toledo, Ohio, and the necessary technology in its evolution is the lawn mower. Proving this simple thesis, however, is not a simple matter. Let's begin with some of the problems that one faces when inquiring into the history of things that we take for granted.

Part One

The Philistine Effect and Other Challenges in Researching Vernacular Culture

There is the problem of the forest and the trees. Vernacular objects and behaviors are so abundant and pervasive that it seems unnecessary to study what is "always there" and all around us. Possibly the most insidious of problems is that the object of study is *normal*, and all of us, scholars, journalists and the general populace alike, do not attend to normal behaviors. We attend to superlatives and exceptions, the first, best and only, rather than the normal and commonplace. Historical research compounds these problems. Whereas we *can* study contemporary vernacular culture by direct observation, historical research depends upon records. But historical records exist where they have been deemed worthy of recording and preserving, or where they have survived from sheer durability, which places us right back with the problems mentioned before, because potential observers of the commonplace in the past were *also* in the midst of abundant, pervasive, normal and unexceptional cultural behaviors! The situation gets worse the farther we go back, because class-consciousness obscures and distorts the record. Vernacular culture usually appears in the historical record as objects of censure, ridicule, contempt or pity. Much that survives is also distorted by the "Philistine effect." Until recently all we knew of the Philistines was what the Hebrews reported, and their reports are all bad press; this effect marks much of our knowledge of those past vernacular cultures which survive only in the disapproving commentaries of moral, social and aesthetic critics.

The vernacular front yard suffers from all these research problems, particularly as we try to focus on the period of origin of the *generic front yard*, which I will define simply as the *unwalled lawn of a one-family house facing a street or road*. Before the Civil War these do not seem to exist, after 1900 they are the rule.[3] Something happened in that 35-year period, and with rare exceptions, architects, landscape designers, urban planners, social critics, domestic tastemakers and the intelligentsia deplored the open yard and pleaded for privacy. The notable exception was the realtor, Frank Jesup Scott, of whom more will be said later.

More representative is an anonymous contributor to the *Atlantic Monthly* who in 1909 lamented "On Our Fenceless State." A seventh-generation Yankee, she longed for a ten-foot high brick English wall. "As a good, modern American," she wrote, "I ought to rejoice that my grass and rambler roses and golden glow are thine, or anybody's who happens along. We live in a cottage set with many others in one wide, communistic lawn, over which our children collectively and individually, scamper freely.... Bruno and Rover, equipped with twice the number of muddy feet, scamper, too. I suppose the man behind the whirring mower knows where our lawn ends and Mr. Wheaton's begins. *I don't*.... No," she continues, "we have pretended long enough that we own a bit of out-doors. We don't, not one grass-blade, not one pebble." She concludes, "I have heard, I think, below the conventional surface in this neighborhood grumbles of discontent with our fenceless state. I am willing to wager...that we have only to set the example in order to see our English wall flattered by at least half a dozen imitations within the year" (283-284).[4]

We shall return to this, especially the "whirring mower," but I must confess that in quoting these sprightly critiques, I am myself distorting the evidence. This is because I uncovered no more than half-a-dozen titles dealing directly with front-yard aesthetics in a century's volumes of the *Readers' Guide to Periodical Literature*. This is all the more remarkable when one realizes that in 1905 the *Readers' Guide* was obliged to list "Back Yards" as a subject-heading followed shortly after with "Outdoor Rooms," both subject-headings being submerged into "Decks, Patios, Terraces" in 1976. There has never been a need for a "Front Yard" subject heading.[5] Almost every single-family house has one, but nobody cares to write about them. Lawns, however, are a concern of the popular periodicals back into the nineteenth century, but all of the articles have been technical, aimed at an implicit aesthetic standard. As all art is purported to aspire toward the purity of music, all lawns have striven to the purity of Astroturf: uniformly green, smooth, weedless and care-free.[6]

One might inquire about the validity of the *Readers' Guide* as a research tool. We are looking at *vernacular* gardening, not landscape architecture *per se* and so the published primary sources are in popular mass publications rather than professional journals. Even so, is it right to suppose that *The American Home, Better Homes and Gardens, House Beautiful, Ladies' Home Journal, Popular Mechanics, Sunset, Southern Living* and like magazines are 1) read by vernacular gardeners and 2) directly affect what they do? Addressing the first question, we must refine our definition of *vernacularity*. In America, we cannot limit vernacular culture to the illiterate population which is quite small and more properly defined as having *traditional folk culture*.[7] Moreover, a vernacular front yard is by definition attached to a single-family residence, implying a degree of economic security as well as a modicum of free choice in outside decor. Single-family rental units are a special variant (neglectful renters have always been a problem), but home ownership is the norm. A house of one's own is part of the American Dream,[8] and doing-it-yourself has long been part of the American Way of home ownership. Popular periodicals have had a partnership with do-it-yourself American homeowners since the middle of the nineteenth century, not only in those which have been indexed in *Readers' Guide* since 1890 (and its precursor *Poole's Index* reaching back to 1802), but in tabloids such as *Hearth and Home*, farm magazines like *The Prairie Farmer*, unindexed magazines like *Woman's Day* or *Home Handyman*, as well as in free guides provided by seed companies and the Department of Agriculture. It is a big business, and has been for a long time.

The word "business" is not a mere metaphor, for as this history unfolds, it will be seen that the vernacular front yard of America develops in tandem with modern industry and with the mass marketing of everything from the simplest domestic products to the land itself. There are intangible factors as well. The above-mentioned American Dream is one; but I do not perceive any hoary origins for American lawns such as the genetic imprinting from *homo sapiens* earliest homegrounds in the grass-scapes of central Africa. Neither do I find the American yard's origins in the pilgrim fathers' drive to clear the woods, which some believe to be legacy of the medieval fear of the deep, dark forests. If these theories had any validity as causative factors we would not have modern African villages swept clear of all grass (it harbors insects and snakes). Likewise, if the broad clearing around a home were a European "deep structure," all Germany and England would have had American-style front yards long ago. Indeed, we wouldn't have to inquire into the mystery of origins, because the vernacular front yard would be in an uninterrupted continuum from Jamestown and Plimmouth Plantation to this very moment.

No, the medieval heritage is one of walls, walls that put a premium on urban space, forcing houses to the verge of narrow streets, without a hint of front yards. Even more ancient are the courtyard traditions of Mesopotamia and the Mediterranean countries, where gardens are enclosed, not open. It is true, however, that the American front yard does have its stylistic ancestry in the spreading parklands of the English gentry of the early eighteenth century (this will be spelled out in chapter five); thereby connecting with the ancient pastoral artistic tradition. But the translation of aristocratic parks into the vernacular was effected by commerce and technology of the latter nineteenth century. In short, by business. Popular magazines for the mass audience evolved during this same time period, so it is reasonable to search in them for the elusive beginnings of the front yard. But there are problems here, too.

The Philistine Effect and Other Challenges 9

1. Exemplar of the American vernacular front yard at its best: open, neat, lawn without any visible division from the neighbor's, foundation plantings that neither obscure the view from the street nor ensure privacy within; a specimen ornamental tree, and, on the boulevard, newly planted shade trees to replace the victims of Dutch elm disease.

2. In pre-industrial rural societies the yard is an "outdoor living room," if we understand that social and production areas are not greatly differentiated inside or out. Detail of a Haitian village scene by native artist Myrthi Benson.

10 Front Yard America

3. A street in Winchester, England shows how the walled cities of medieval times discouraged wasted space, most certainly for ornamental front yards.

4. The earliest English settlements at Jamestown (here) and Plimmouth replicated medieval manor villages. Not much to suggest antecedents for the vernacular front yard, but the American tradition of single-family detached homes begins here.

The Philistine Effect and Other Challenges

5. In areas settled by Spanish and French, the Mediterranean courtyard tradition contrasts with English and northern U.S. traditions. The Governor's Palace in San Antonio presents a rather unwelcome façade. In Europe, North Africa and Asia Minor these front the streets without any yard space. This building, however, probably was within a walled compound like the neighboring missions.

6. The in-turning courtyard area of the Governor's Palace makes for a very private outdoor living room. What about poorer town dwellers who lived in tenement apartments? Their yards were public plazas at markets, fountains and churches.

12 Front Yard America

7. Of constant charm to American tourists are England's "flower basket" front yards. The commonalities with Americans are single-family homes and a degree of set-back from the road (fairly pronounced here in Penzance along the waterfront), but the use of solid dividing walls, the preference for flowers over grass, and the completely individualistic style for each yard are an ocean apart.

8. Where is this? Every characteristic of the American vernacular is here, but this is a trio of residences in Birmingham, England, set in a district of English vernacular: row houses with low-walled front gardens and detached homes totally invisible behind eight-foot walls of brick, stone or boards. It is only through such startling departures from national norms that we can recognize that we, too, speak a dialect!

The Philistine Effect and Other Challenges

9. In the 1920s and 1930s British landscape architects strove vainly to change the English vernacular toward the neater American style. Said one team of landscapers, "It is enough to bring tears to the eyes of the designer of houses to see what should be a simple lawn mutilated by constellations of flower beds."

14 Front Yard America

10. The vernacular style is national. Aerial of a New Orleans neighborhood with narrow lots, front yards separated only by driveways, and at the bottom, a sequence of keeping-up-with-the Joneses pools. Only one has crossed the street, suggesting how important immediate proximity can be to diffusion of innovations.

11. The American style is as pronounced in the country as in the suburbs. This Illinois farm is protected on the north by a thick shelter-belt, yet the lawn extends onto the highway right-of-way. Would there have been a shelter belt if the house faced north?

The Philistine Effect and Other Challenges 15

12. The long driveways in this development in rural western Wisconsin bespeak withdrawal into privacy yet, of 26 residences 22 have open, front vistas. Two others have extensive yard plantings, and the last two are hidden in the grove of trees on the left.

13. Atlanta, being in the Appalachian foothills, has natural features that can make the contiguous vistas difficult to achieve but, wherever possible, the open vernacular predominates.

16 Front Yard America

14. Historic districts of Galveston, Texas are bringing back elegant fences, but the standard vernacular yard prevails in more recent neighborhoods.

15. Not quite so conformist as you might think, a house-by-house tally of this block on Minnesota's Iron Range showed quite individual choices and placement of a wide variety of flowers, shrubs, trees and ornaments. Nonetheless, the message is not *liberté*, but *egalité*.

Part Two

Learning About Front Yards from the Critics

No matter how popular the periodical, the overall tenor of the articles on landscaping in this century has been elite, suburban and spacious. *House Beautiful, The Craftsman* and *Country Life* were downright snobbish and few of their ideas could be applied to 50-foot lots. Furthermore, most of the authors in all periodicals are landscape architects who never take on low-budget do-it-yourself clients, and who usually regard the vernacular front yard as an endemic disease, blots upon the landscape and personal offenses to sensitive eyes. The single exception proves the rule. One of America's leading landscape architects of the first half of the twentieth century, Harold A. Caparn, addressed "The Average Yard; The Story of a Fifty-Foot Lot" during The Great Depression "because the larger and more lucrative houses and grounds are at present so scarce. So," he adds tellingly, "the *most interesting* house and lot nowadays are those that meet the needs of the Average Man and Woman" (42).[9] I've emphasized "most interesting" because except for the extreme hard times of 1937, the average yard and 50-foot lot have had no professional interest whatsoever during the twentieth century. Even such a fetching title as "Smaller Spaces: Six Success Stories" in a 1989 *Garden Design* magazine is elite, not vernacular, dealing with such smaller spaces as a Chicago penthouse and a Manhattan "yard."

More representative of professional views is Elizabeth Gordon's ten-year campaign to reform the American domestic landscape. It is worth examining closely because it contains perceptive historical analyses about yards and gardens, and because it was a conscious attempt to foment a revolution in front yards. Gordon, the editor of *House Beautiful*, devoted 34 pages of the February 1951 issue to the question "When is a garden American Style?" She wrote:

Originally, the traditional American garden was the front lawn. [Quite erroneous, as we shall see.] It was the true expression of the spiritual attitudes of our people. Each householder maintained his front yard for the enjoyment of everybody, and was permitted to enjoy everyone else's in return. As a result no one felt envious or shut out. Each identified himself with the whole. This was a reflection of our social attitudes. These friendly extroverted gardens had their part in forming the friendly extroverted people, who are our finest product. But that kind of garden had no privacy and was not used as a room.

The new American garden keeps this friendly, open character, but strives for privacy as well. We live closer together these days, our streets are no longer quiet thoroughfares and our houses are smaller. (55)

The social and technological changes that caused America to invent "its *own* Style in Gardens" were neatly summarized in the same issue by *House Beautiful's* Garden Editor, Dr. Joseph E. Howland. These influences, Howland said, produced certain American Style garden behaviors:

*permanent ground-patterns to banish off-seasons
*evergreens predominating as important planting
*"wonderful plants" for dramatic accents
*paved areas where grass won't grow
*mowing strips to save work—"Modern America doesn't have time for hand-trimming, so eliminates the need for it"
*play space for children (76-79)

Informality, naturalness, interlocking indoor-outdoor design, greatly reduced flower-beds, privacy for outdoor recreation and leisure are the characteristics and goals. If it sounds Californian, it is: "The new American Style garden came into full flower on the West Coast about 1935." If it sounds like Frank Lloyd Wright, it is—Wright, Maybeck, and Greene and Greene were the pioneers early in the century (Gordon, "A Garden" 58, 152). And if it sounds as if Gordon and Howland were correct about the trends in professional American landscape architecture for the ensuing 40 years—again, you're right on target. There really *is* an American style, which dominates all professionally designed gardens, as well as sumptuous books like Architectural Digest's *Gardens* and Ken Druse's *The Natural Garden*, periodical articles from *Fine Gardening* to *Woman's Day*, and popular do-it-yourself guides by Sunset, Ortho and Burpees.

All true, and yet by the end of the decade Elizabeth Gordon recognized that her ultimate goal was not a yard closer. The "American Style" had made no inroads on the 50-Foot Lot. Moreover, Average Man and Woman proved incorrigible.[10] Gordon removed the velvet gloves. "Does Your Front Lawn Belong to You—or the Whole Neighborhood?" was the challenging title of a May 1960 article. "The front yard is a symbol," she said, "the best symbol of the whole issue of whether your land is yours.... The issue really boils down to whether or not others have a right to look at or onto your land. Is each man's property his, or is it visually his neighbors'? Have you the right to eat breakfast on the terrace in your pajamas, or is that committing a community nuisance?" (152). What really irked her is that people were giving the wrong answers. The previous summer her staff had interviewed "home owners in areas where outdoor privacy is not known and where it is commonly held that a neighbor's land is common property visually." Here is what they said:

*I want people to see what my house looks like.
*I want to know what my neighbors are doing.
*People want to see the open vistas across the yards.
*I like to look out and see what's happening.
*It's prettier to drive through a street with wide front lawns.
*It's the custom in our town.

How can the people be so wrong-headed? Gordon's answer can be easily summarized. They are the victims of conspiracy! The conspiracy began "40 to 60 years ago" (circa 1900-1920) with the big real estate developers who "rebelled against the row-house practices of eastern cities like Boston, Philadelphia, Baltimore and New York," and began to develop park-like suburbs with only large parcels of land and deeds calling for "deep setbacks and low fences and hedges." This aesthetic was thereupon superimposed on smaller parcels by ordinances that rendered a *neighborhood* of adjoining independent homes into a designed estate. The result is that homeowners really don't own their front yard. "The majority of the established residential areas in the United States are ruled by deed restrictions or zoning ordinances which say what you must or must not do with your land. They say how far back from the street and the sidelines the house must be. And they prescribe whether or not fences may be built and, if so, how high and what materials, and even how dense; for example, whether they must be see-throughable, etc." As Gordon's 1951 articles seemed to foreshadow the 1950s of Ozzie and Harriet and the Beach Boys, this article is a bellwether of the 1960s. Organize the neighborhood, she says, challenge the laws, use the system to get variances, and if these fail, use "the gentle art of evasion" with hedge, vines and berms rather than fences, or by erecting privacy fences within your property rather than on the boundaries (152, 232-234). Upper-crust homeowners of the world, unite!

Undoubtedly there is some validity to the conspiracy theory of front yard aesthetics. Landscape architects, real estate developers and city fathers conspired to foist upon the homeowners a common plan that satisfied the powers that were, but thwarted personal taste. The very fact that there are ordinances restricting fence building assures us that local governments enforce a standard of landscape beauty.[11] Most certainly the legal restrictions have frustrated not only individually deviant tastes but revolutionary schemes of urban designers.

The conspiracy goes only so far, though. Consider *rural* front yards. They are not subject to realty scams or to civic ordinances, and even on farms where fields that adjoin the yard are not pastured, there may not be so much as a barbed wire fence. Rural front lawns are likely to be clipped right up to the frontage road. We can only conclude that this is a style that people *liked*, that they felt *right* about. Elizabeth Gordon's fulmination chose not to accept the homeowner's satisfaction with their open front yards. But we should ask, are these householders mere dupes? Or are they victims of self-delusion such as serfs, slaves and the disenfranchised have been for millennia, gratefully accepting things "as they are"? There is something in this; as J.B. Jackson has suggested, vernacular styles are the product of "making do" with givens.[12] We might characterize the thought process, as "the law says I can't have a fence so I'll see what I can make of a yard without one. Having done so, I like it. It's my style. It's the way things should be." Duplicity? Self-delusion? Intelligent accommodation? Or the expression of a life-style? My own response is to recognize and accept the truth that determinism operates in all life-styles, that accommodation to the inevitable is a sensible trait of reasonable beings, and that custom gives content. And yet, there's more. A quarter-century after *House Beautiful* surveyed front-yard attitudes, Christopher Grampp surveyed 50 San Francisco Bay area residents—most of them professionals who had lived in their current homes for 10-20 years—and these people, who enjoyed California-style *backyard* lives, were almost militant in their support of the fenceless, public, "un-used" front yard. Like Grampp, I choose to take people at their word on matters of aesthetics. These folks know what they like. The supercilious response to "I know what I like" ("No, you like what you know") sometimes misses the point about vernacular tastes. What people *know* may actually be profound, true and beautiful in terms of mythic fundamentals of national values. "It's the custom in our town," said one of *House Beautiful's* interviewees in 1959. One of Christopher Grampp's Californians put it simply: the front yard is "just for other people to see." Indeed, Elizabeth Gordon's introductory remarks to her 1951 article hit the nail on the head: The front lawn was—*and is*—"the true expression of the spiritual attitudes of our people" (40-42).[13]

What about the need for privacy and the ideal of the grounds "as extension of indoor living" (Gordon's phrase for the American Style)? The sequence of subject headings to periodical literature indicate that since the establishment of "communistic" front lawn, the front porch, the back yard, the outdoor living room in back, the terrace, patio and deck have been paramount concerns among homeowners.

Returning to a question that I raised several pages back as to whether magazine articles actually influence vernacular patterns, the answer is yes. But the influence is characterized by *piecemeal adaptation* and *diffusion of innovations*. Ideas and plans are not followed wholly, and in most cases they can't be. Affordable, do-able, available and generally scaled-down innovations are selected and incorporated by one person in a neighborhood, and if it is appealing, it diffuses. This can be tested by direct observation. If you see one front yard "fencelet," you will be able to see variations on this theme for a city block or so. The usual pattern can be plotted as a symmetrical rising and falling curve with the most pronounced example in the middle. Fences, for instance, often show a yard completely enclosed by see-throughable chain-link fence, neighbored by lesser chain link fences (sometimes not even enclosing any space), adjoining low picket fences and finally trailing off to a miniature split-rail defining a front corner—and then to contiguous lawns until another token fencelet appears. If you fly, observe the patterns of turquoise pools in suburban back yards. Olympic in the center, inflatable waders at the peripheries. I will return to diffusion of innovations in the larger context of lawn technology, but let us inquire now into the evolution of the vernacular front yard.

Learning About Front Yards 25

16. How did front yards look before the Civil War? Connors Prairie reconstructed village of circa 1849 has houses directly fronting the streets, with enclosed kitchen gardens.

17. The Tullie Smith House Restoration of the Atlanta Historical Society attempts to reconstruct a pre-lawn front yard. The closely-ranked pickets enclose a garden of vegetables, simples and flowers. To us this seems ornamental, but actually it is practical.

26 Front Yard America

18. This circa 1865 view on Nicollet Island on the Mississippi in Minneapolis shows newly planted shade trees on the boulevard of a nascent street. A.J. Downing noted deprecatingly in 1859 that such plantings are on the "beau-ideal of...newly-planned villages." (Minnesota Historical Society)

19. From the 1874 Atlas of Sangamon County Illinois, the "late residence of R.H. Constant" is at once a primer on fencing and a caution about trusting such views. The croquet-players in the "outer court" share the grounds with a small herd, but overall it is clear that by means of new board fencing along the road, and a picket enclosure, the house presents a public ornament, and is combining the requirements of farming with the aristocratic ideal of a pleasure ground. We are left unenlightened about lawn care, but it seems likely that the inner yard would be clipped with a lawnmower, and the outer grazed. Note the insert of the Old Homestead, where undifferentiated uses prevailed. (Illinois State Historical Library)

Learning About Front Yards 27

20. From the same atlas, a rare view showing work (the woman is feeding chickens) and realistic disorder (a pile of branches waiting to be chopped). (Illinois State Historical Society)

21. Although undated, these three Indiana views epitomize the progression of front yards from pioneering to the modern day. In the first, a substantial fence of hand-hewn picket protects fruit trees and shrubs and possibly a garden. The original one-room log cabin's brick chimney has deteriorated suggesting a passage of years from the 1940s to 1860s. In front of the three-generation family appear to be two raised garden beds; the area is probably enclosed within a cattle fence. (The Brandt house. Indiana Historical Society Library Negative #C4298)

28 Front Yard America

22. Here, the front yard has become at least an incipient outdoor "living room." The immediate front has no kitchen garden; to the left is a grape arbor, to the right apple trees. The front entrance is not mere access: the steps and boardwalk will keep mud and dust out. The sidelights and transom imply a parlor within. The pickets are of dressed lumber, and while one finial is incomplete, this is a facade presented with pride. The grass is not edged and is rough cut. (Samuel & Margaret Miller House. Indiana Historical Society Library Negative #C2161)

Learning About Front Yards 29

23. The transformation to modernity is complete in this photograph. Everything speaks of material self-satisfaction. The brightly painted Queen Anne house has a veritable "cadillac" porch. The tasselled flynet, the brass lamps on the phaeton, the lady's stylish tailored suit are the height of fashion in 1897 catalogs. What has happened to the fence? It has moved onto the porch, an invitation rather than a barrier. The mowed lawn is a summer living room; a lawn chair is visible over the lady's shoulder. The poster in the window suggests these are the ladies of a political home. (Indiana Historical Society Library Negative #C4297)

Part Three

Living in Front Yards and Back Yards

In the beginning, front yards were outdoor living rooms. That is to say, under primitive conditions a dwelling houses a variety of social and economic activities which, depending upon the weather, spill outside. This is especially true of food preparation in hot weather, not only for cooking, but for shelling peas and peeling spuds while keeping an eye on children and neighbors (if there are any), and tossing the leavings to the family fowl and swine. Evidence of such extensions of indoor living can be acquired second-hand at outdoor living history museums of pioneer life, from photographs of western pioneer homes, and from direct observation of primitive and economically deprived villages, reservations and barrios worldwide. Yards are usually grassless (often by design), generally littered, and shared equally by people, pets, chickens and, frequently, pigs.[14] The next stage is an enclosure, a chicken-proof fence that implies a kitchen garden within. From this point, the historical record of vernacular yards is thin, obscure and speculative. Christie White, horticulturist and researcher at the Old Sturbridge Village living history museum has described the difficulty of "Documenting and Interpreting Early 19th Century Rural Gardens at Old Sturbridge Village." There are no photographs as sources for an early nineteenth-century reconstruction, so landscape paintings, genre paintings and illustrations must be used, but they are subject to artistic license. Also, they often show fences but not what is behind them, and in the majority of cases depict more affluent and progressive homes and yards. Garden advice literature was published in accelerating abundance in Massachusetts in the 1830s, but, White says, this is also suspect for researching typicality because it often tells what *should* be, not what is. For our purpose of looking at front yards, garden literature is virtually useless because the topics are horticultural rather than architectural. There is also the Philistine Effect. White quotes an article from an 1837 issue of *New England Farmer*: "Nothing is more indubitably indicative of the husbandry of the farm and the order of the house, than the condition of the front yard...with its fences broken down, gates unhung, and its interior littered up with old shoes, dead cats, broken jugs, etc..." (189-190). This sort of criticism of front yards continues into the twentieth century. Frederick L. Allen writing of "Our National Shabbiness" in a 1915 *House Beautiful* describes the fictional return of an American prodigal who sees in towns "a superfluity of straggling, unpainted wooden fences, of scrawny telegraph-poles, of dingy front-yards, which obtrude themselves upon the most favorable compositions" (34).[15] In 1948, Ottalie K. Williams titled a one-paragraph column in *The American Home* "Your Grounds Are *Everybody's* Business," because "A house set among weeds, straggly vines, and pock-marked lawns is a poor advertisement for both its owners and their environment" and she recalled "two elderly maiden ladies who turned 'queer' in their later years" letting the garden become "a jungle of weeds and brambles. The old ladies stick by what they consider their rights and do nothing about it. And all the neighbors can do is put up high, split chestnut fences to shut out the ugly sight." The fence, notice, is a *last resort* defense against neighbors who have unbalanced the equilibrium between rights and responsibilities (22).[16]

Back yards have been subject to much more aggressive campaigns. Here we *can* point to Joshuas tumbling the walls, right in the midst of the City Beautiful Movement (a national groundswell that aimed to give more coordinated civic design in the manner of the "White City" of the 1893 Chicago Columbian Exposition). In 1916 New York's Tenement House Committee of the Charity Organization Society circularized tenement landlords and builders with a pamphlet having two pictures, "one showing a typical block of the hideous high board fences; and the other, yards separated by neat, trim metal fences, encouraging the transformation of bare grounds and open areas into grass plots, flower beds and play places ("Metal Fences" 172). A "Beautify Baltimore" Committee, formed in 1910, had succeeded in reforming the back yards of Baltimore's famous row houses, "so that the whole effect is of one long 'block garden,' and the pleasant greenery and blossoms of each home may be enjoyed by all the neighbors" (H. James 577). The New York campaign was couched in the economic terms of real estate conspirators, while Baltimore was more concerned with the moral uplift of the teeming masses. Either way, these are backyards in intensely urban areas. But also either way, these are indictments of the high board fences that apparently predominated in older city neighborhoods both tenement and established. The two most famous corner lots in America—those of the lawyers J.M. Clemens in Hannibal, Missouri and A. Lincoln in Springfield, Illinois—suggest that boarded-up back yards were normal in smaller towns too (Curtis; Ward). Francis Guy's paintings of the village of Brooklyn on Long Island prior to 1820 disclose some of the fenced functions of stable, chicken yard and privy (Flexner 44; cf "Growth of Cities" 172). John Jakle's *The American Small Town: Twentieth-Century Place Images* describes these totally functional "backyards of low-income people fenced with well-trodden paths leading from the back or side door to the privy, barn, and other outbuildings," and he also finds evidence of unsightly clutter as the rule (56-57). As late as 1940, *Good Housekeeping* would ask "What Does Your *Neighbor* See?" advocating little corrals, picket fences and trellises to mask garbage cans (142). Rural back yards are notorious eyesores; wherever there are adjacent barns and outbuildings the jetsam of agriculture accumulates. In two important circulars of the University of Illinois Agricultural Experiment Station (1914, 1915) Wilhelm Miller addressed farmyard clutter in *The Illinois Way of Beautifying the Farm*. The "Illinois Way" of screening unsightly objects is to hide them behind wind breaks, or to cover them with vines of wild cucumber, trumpet-creeper or wild grape, or "dig up enough elder and sumac from the roadside to make the outbuildings decent without delay" ("The Illinois Way" 170, 4-5).

Cleaning up back yards and opening them to neighborhood scrutiny is one thing; converting them to private living space is another because a sacred icon, the front porch, had to be sacrificed. "Back Yard *versus* Front Porch" set the battle line, at least in well-to-do suburban life of House Beautiful in 1922. "All through the West and Middle West," wrote Esther Johnson, "where towns were built in the front-porch period, attention is turning to the garden in the back yard. The family moves its chairs to the back to avoid watching the never-ceasing procession of automobile headlights...and plants hedges to give a little more privacy." Johnson, however, was not thinking of the repellent back yards described above; she writes nostalgically of childhood memories of grassy yards, where one lay "face up through drowsy afternoons and watched odd humped clouds in a blue sky, and heard the hum of bees in the June roses, and felt and smelled the lush grass.... there is sanity in the child's love of the earth and the child's dislike for that artificial substitute—the front porch." Three years later, the attack on front porches was in full swing. Describing "How I Did It," i.e. removed the porch, Edith Dunham Smith sarcastically dismissed porches as things that in the "dark ages before the advent of the car" provided an "accurate method of gauging the exact financial status of people living in the county." So porches were "Ford, Buick and Rolls-Royce" symbols of wealth. By 1940, an American Home reader complained of the "epidemic of lopping off front porches," and in the early 1950s, there were wistful articles on "How to Handle a Useless Porch," on the "Passing of the Old Front Porch," "What Can You Do With a Front Porch?," "We Miss Our Front Porch," the "Eclipse of the Family Porch," and from Collier's, a melancholy "Goodbye, Old Friend."

All of this relates to the evolution of the front yard from full living space to public ornament. The pioneer front yard, as we have seen, was an extended work area. A fence was necessary to keep free-roaming animals out (and/or domestic fowl in). As families prospered and as Victorians specialized domestic space, the living room lost its economic activities, and the front yard likewise converted to space for family leisure and social intercourse, but with two signs of privacy (or more accurately, *transitional zones*); one, the front porch, the other, the friendly fence (of which more later). At the same time, back yards retained their utilitarian functions (the term "clothes yard" was commonly used) and were often boarded up for privacy in drying clothes and hair, as genteel Esther Johnson said, but also for privies and keeping chickens. Back yards lost much of their utility early in the twentieth century. Indoor plumbing was certainly a major factor, and John Jakle points out "as the automobile had greatly stimulated the money economy at the expense of traditional forms of barter and subsistence, hen houses, barns, woodsheds, gardens and orchards disappeared from behind houses. Backyards were cleaned up in the more affluent neighborhoods" (138). The back yard gradually took over the outdoor living room functions of the front porch, and the front yard was left with only symbolic meaning.

Following the Civil War the historical record improves because of photography, illustrated county atlases and bird's-eye view maps.[17] The upper class bias continues, of course, but one can search for the more modest-sized houses and lots. The "friendly fence" predominates—low, see-throughable wooden pickets, cast iron or horizontal boards. Judging from the bird's-eye maps and county atlases, landscaping of the more spacious yards of the midwest appears to be limited to lawns and ungrouped trees with few shrubs and no flower beds or foundation plantings. The absence of floral ornament seems to have been true of New England as well, for in 1881 short story writer Sarah Orne Jewett mourned the disappearance of enclosed front yard gardens, "different from the rest of the land altogether." Alice Morse Earle, who quotes Jewett in her 1927 *Old Time Gardens; A Book of the Sweet O the Year*, is one of the rare writers on gardens who wants to fill the front dooryard with a riot of floral color. "When the fences disappeared with the night rambles of the cows, the front yards changed character; the tender blooms vanished, but the tall shrubs and the Peonies and the Flower de Luce sturdily grew and blossomed, *save where that dreary destroyer of a garden crept in the desire for a lawn*" (38-41).[18]

Unfortunately, no matter how valuable atlases and maps may be as sources for urban history, they are most suspect in exactly the details that we want. John Reps' monumental *Views and Viewmakers of Urban America* demonstrates that by and large these are accurate lithographs (inaccuracy would not have sustained an industry of bird's-eye views of over 2,400 cities and towns and untold illustrations in county atlases), but the existence and condition of fences and yards is especially subject to artistic license. A virulent expose of the industry, published in 1879 and quoted by Reps described the sales pitch to a home owner thus:

Our plan is, to have an artist of acknowledged ability visit you, Mr. Jones—in case you accept—and make the drawings from nature. In this way, any changes or improvements you may contemplate making in the future can be made in the sketch.... For instance, you would want that pile of wood near your house out of the sketch, and the rubbish about the back-yard, which you are about to cart off, should not appear. You had better have a picket fence in front, instead of those rails, as you undoubtedly will have a picket fence there some day.... Of course we can make your house look as though it had just been painted, and we can put a grass lawn in front. A few evergreen trees would look well. (69)

The images of specific homes, therefore, are as likely to be subjunctive rather than declarative statements. The writer of the passage clearly has an ax to grind, but more objective studies support the contention. A few years ago the Historical Department of the Mormon Church did an exhaustive block-by-block study of an 1870 view of Salt Lake City, and while finding the views "highly accurate," it eliminated many buildings and "fences, light poles and other smaller items" (Reps 72). I have examined an 1883 bird's-eye view of Duluth, Minnesota, finding only *two* fenced yards in a city of 13,000! The few relevant photographs from the period indicate there were some horizontal board fences at this time, though not many. Not surprisingly, these panoramic views seem to have rather standardized vernacular housing, partly because it really was standardized, but mostly because the urban views were paid for by subscribers whose businesses and homes were given detailed attention. All the vignettes in the county atlases of the 1860-1920 vintage are those of subscribers, so modest dwellings are rare. As for actual photographs of streets, yards and houses, (and except for pioneer farms, these are uncommon until 1890) artistic license is not so free, and yet picture-taking is usually an occasion when one carefully sets the record straight, telling truths as they should be known. The very *best* truths one can achieve, just like the "truthful views" of homes and grounds in today's *Architectural Digest* and *Garden Design* where compost heaps, tricycles, hoses and lawnmowers are never to be seen.

Part Four

The Coming of the Lawn Mower

Let us not throw out the baby with the bath water, though. However scanty the evidence, it is clear that fences of some sort *were* the common pattern through 1875-1880 with specimen trees planted randomly around the yard in what we might call a "Downing-realist style." Andrew Jackson Downing (1815-1852) revolutionized American taste through his popular books on landscape gardening and country residences and his editorship of *The Horticulturist* magazine. Downing's spirit looms like an all-embracing spectre over American landscape architecture from the 1840s to the present day, but as his writings are directed at rural estates rather than modest farms and city streets, they are of slight direct relevance. As we shall see, though, indirectly he set the direction for the vernacular yard. Norman Newton has criticized the discrepancy between Downing's words and execution. He did "assemble fine collections of trees that in the course of time naturally became stately" against their spectacular Hudson valley backdrops, but the illustrations to his books seem spotty and undesigned (264-265). The farm and town yards in county atlases of Illinois and Indiana look like this, but whether or not they were trying to vitalize diagrams from Downing, Holly and others, or just planting exotic trees, we cannot say for certain. The latter is probably the case, because Wilhelm Miller in his "Illinois Way" and "Prairie Spirit" pamphlets of 1914-1915 castigated untutored homeowners on many grounds: "any beginner can put flowerbeds in the middle of the lawn...[trying]...to make each dollar stand up on edge where everyone can see it" ("The Illinois Way" 2). The "Illinois way" is to use permanent native species of shrubs and trees that grow wild in Illinois for at least 90 percent of all plantings on farms and 80 percent in cities. Give the house a background, Miller says, frame the view of your house, improve the view from your porch, keep the open lawn free of a peppering of flowers, plant shrub borders rather than hedges or beds, hide the house foundation with shrubs and above all, resist the Colorado blue spruce and those "vegetable exclamation marks," the Lombardy poplars. There are rewards—the pamphlet was free to anyone "who will sign a promise to do some permanent ornamental planting within a year," and throughout, Miller hammers at enhanced real estate values ("The Illinois Way" 5-9).

Miller's enthusiastic and practical circulars tell us much of vernacular yards early in the twentieth century. My examination of photographs of houses in central Illinois 1895-1905 corroborates some things, makes others questionable. Foundation plantings are rare, as are shrubs. Lawns are clipped, fenceless and not at all "peppered" with flowers. Indeed, of 41 houses, only 17 had *any* ornamental shrubs or flowers, and all but five were sparse. The one real exception is an Italianate brick house, the elegant Gehrmann residence of Springfield. It is the only truly landscaped estate. Photographs of 1901 show a veritable jungle of birches, pines, palms, willows, shrubs, and vines interspersed with broad graveled walks—and remarkably shaggy lawns.

These lawns are anachronistic, for they are truly Downing style lawns, untouched by the technological revolution of the lawn mower, which is the invisible force in nearly every other house photo I've examined for the period following the Civil War. It should be recognized that maintenance of a smooth short lawn without a mechanical mower is extremely labor intensive. Sheep, of course, provide the model for pastoral perfection, and they were the lawn mowers for the great estates of England. With the development of ha-ha's as a means of keeping sheep away from the immediate house environs, the broad sweep of lawn was possible without fencing as such. But how were those swards cared for where sheep's unseemly propensities for eating everything within reach and depositing manure at random were unwanted? The answer is the scythe. (See headpiece, Part One.)

The Coming of the Lawn Mower

In 1846, Downing devoted "A Chapter on Lawns" for the American readers of *The Horticulturist*. "There are but few good lawns yet in America," he says, "...but they are rapidly multiplying." The process of properly developing the proper soil is detailed, and then:

> After your lawn is once fairly established, there are but two secrets in keeping it perfect—frequent mowing and rolling. Without the first, it will soon degenerate into a coarse meadow; the latter will render it firmer, closer, shorter, and finer every time it is repeated.
>
> A good lawn must be mown every ten days or fortnight. The latter may be assumed as the proper average time in this climate. Ten days is the usual limit of growth for the best kept lawns in England, and it is surprising how soon a coarse and wiry bit of sward will become smooth turf, under the magic influences of regular and oft repeated mowing and rolling.
>
> Of course, a lawn can only be cut when the grass is damp, and rolling is best performed directly after rain. The English always roll a few hours before using the scythe. On large lawns, a donkey or light horse may be advantageously employed in performing this operation. (185-186)

Downing doesn't mention the existence of the machine lawn mowers which had been patented in England by Edward Budding in 1830. (See headpiece, Part Two) Of this, the manufacturer John Ferrabee of Stroud stated that "as the machine can be used best in dry weather, the gardener is enabled to cut his lawns at the most convenient time, instead of being obliged, as with a scythe, to wait for rain or heavy dews" (*Coldwell Lawn Mowers* 10). J.C. Loudon's influential *Encyclopedia of Gardening* contained a cut of Budding's mowing machine, describing it as "an admirable contrivance for cropping, or shearing lawns, grass-plots, or indeed any kind of short grass" (555). Downing would have been familiar with this, and when he visited England in 1850, quite probably saw a mowing machine. He may not have been impressed:

although the Loudon illustration shows a top-hatted gent (no navvy he) pushing the mower, the reality was that it "usually required at least two men to operate a 16-inch [wide] machine" (Coldwell Lawn Mowers 10). There seems also to have been some disdain for lawn machinery. G.M. Kern, whose *Practical Landscape Gardening* of 1853 owed much to Downing, remarked after reiterating the importance of free use of scythe and roller, that "the borders must always be nicely trimmed":

> Many little contrivances have been invented, and may be found in seed stores, for the purpose of facilitating the labor of trimming grass borders. These are most properly left to ladies and children. A sharp spade, and a steady eye and hand, are all that is necessary to trim the neatest border. (123)

What these little contrivances may have been, we do not know (possibly hand shears? See headpiece, Part Seven.), but it is chronicled that the first lawn mower in America belonged to H.W. Sargent of Fishkill, New York, a few miles across the Hudson River from Downing's place in Newburgh. We know this, because the machine (which was sent to Sargent in the "early fifties" by an English friend in Surrey) broke down. Sargent sent it to a machine shop in Newburgh to be repaired, but a machinist, Thomas Coldwell, chose to make a new one. The machine shop thereupon began to manufacture mowers. This monopoly did not revolutionize the landscape; production never exceeded "two hundred lawn mowers in any one year" into the late 1860s (*Coldwell Lawn Mowers* 10-11). By contrast, looking ahead a dozen years, in 1880, 47,661 American lawn mowers were manufactured ("Lawn Mowers,")[20] and by 1913, the Coldwell Company alone was shipping out 700 lawn mowers per nine-hour day (46).[21] Clearly, the decade of the 1870s was when the lawn mower came into its own, and with it, the revolution of the front yard.

As with all revolutions in life styles, the causes are several and subtle. There was one professional advocate of connected

The Coming of the Lawn Mower

front yards, Frank Jesup Scott of Toledo, of whom much more later. Also, in mid-nineteenth century, "laws became ever more restrictive and specific about the necessity of erecting and maintaining fences," gradually, after 1870, shifting the responsibility for keeping animals *in* replacing the necessity for the homeowners' keeping them *out* (Noble 118). This decade also saw the rapid replacement of vernacular farm fencing with much more effective barbed wire—from five tons made and sold in 1874 to over 40,000 tons in 1880 (Dary 315).[22] This would not only have had a salubrious effect on the yards of small towns and villages where the majority of the nation's people resided, but in the rapidly expanding subdivisions being carved out of farmland around cities like Chicago. These subdivisions, as John Stilgoe points out, were, in the 1870s and 1880s, becoming increasingly proletarian, with smaller lots and rectilinear street grids (Stilgoe, *Borderland* esp. Ch. 13 and 152). The suburb movement was as much as a half-century old in 1870, but it accelerated because of expanded commuter lines of horse-trolleys and steam railways, at the same time that the need for cattle-proof and pig-proof residential fences was eliminated. The stage was set, but lawn mowers needed improvements before they were suited for owners of smaller lots.

The key to the needed improvement was to break loose from traditional lawn care—the scythe and the roller. The Englishman Budding had liberated thinking from the motion of the scythe as a model; his mower had a reel or cylinder of spiral knives that rotated against a fixed anvil or "wiper" or "deadknife." Essentially, it actually is an adaptation of the principle of the scythe and the sickle as the sweep of a curved knife cuts one blade of grass at a time (there had been a 1799 English patent for a grain mower that spun a horizontal wheel of four sickles, a design, incidentally, anticipated by Leonardo da Vinci's grim human reaper), but placing these into an Archimedes screw which was powered from the forward motion of wheels was truly innovative, and until post-World

48 Front Yard America

War II, it was the dominant model. Not the only one, however, because the dominant *agricultural* design had saw-toothed reciprocating cutters. A curious adaptation of this principle is an 1863 design (U.S. Patent #38,381) for a one-man grass-cutter where the power for the reciprocating motion is supplied by the operator's turning a geared hand crank while pushing the bar forward. (See headpiece, Part Four.)

1909. *Budding's mowing machine (fig. 513.)* is an admirable contrivance for cropping, or shearing lawns, grass-plots, or indeed any kind of short grass. In the operation of

513

pushing forward the machine, the cylinder (*a*) rolls upon the ground like the wheel of a wheelbarrow; and, by the wheels and pinions connected with it, causes the revolving cutters to act rapidly, by their smooth outer edges, against the edge of the fixed rectangular steel plate (*c*), so as to crop or shear the grass or vegetable surface. The smaller cylinder (*b*) serves effectually to regulate the height, and to ensure the steadiness of the rectangular fixed cutter (*c*), against which the revolving cutters act. To keep the small roller (*b*) sufficiently free from any adhering substances, there is a horizontal box which serves as an axis for a thin iron scraper, which is curved so as to form a portion of a cylinder, having its lower edge bearing on the surface of the roller. There is a box (*d*) in which all the grass cut by the machine is collected, thus saving the expense of sweeping. The machine may be easily rolled from one place to another without cutting by merely lowering the handles, so as to lift the gauge-roller from the ground. Another mowing machine of larger dimensions is occasionally used for mowing extensive lawns.

24. J.C. Loudon's influential *Encyclopedia of Gardening* (1850) spoke well of the first lawn mower (invented 20 years earlier), but in reality it was heavy, unwieldy, and usually required a gardener and boy to move it through the sward.

The Coming of the Lawn Mower

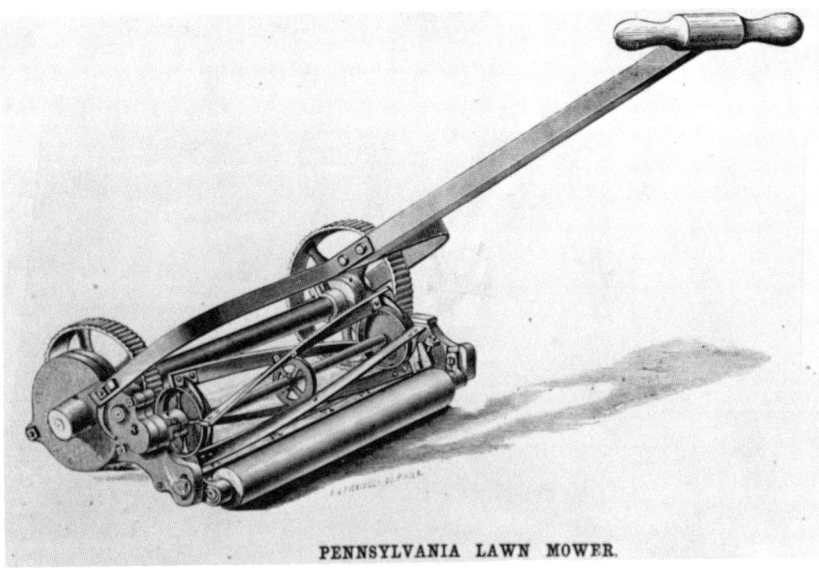

PENNSYLVANIA LAWN MOWER.

25. Thomas Coldwell made the first American lawn mower, copying the design of the only Budding machine in America around 1856. Not many of the heavy machines were manufactured. The breakthrough came in 1869 and 1870 with several lightweight models, particularly "The Pennsylvania."

26. A Budding-style mower persists on an Oxford college quad (1991). The heavy rollers contribute to the putting-green surface. English conservatism about lawn mower innovation was acknowledged as early as 1874 when Manchester's Follows & Bate allowed "there are occasional purchasers who will remain in favor of Lawn Mowers" of this type, rather than their prize-winning Anglo-American model.

50 Front Yard America

27. Significantly, the first lightweight mowers in England were labeled Anglo-American. Girls (never women) showed how easily the new mowers were handled. The 10-inch "Croquet" might be "for a ladies use" and the 14-inch for "where only one man is kept," but all larger sizes had an extra handle for "a lad or man" to pull. In this 1874 catalog Follows & Bate boasted sales of 20,000 in "the past four years." (Courtesy, the Winterthur Library: Printed Book and Periodicals Collection)

The Coming of the Lawn Mower

28a. This 1880 catalog for Blair & Fiske's of Springfield Massachusetts. "Easy" model suggests a mower we're still waiting for. Not only "highly favored with Children and Ladies as well as some lazy men," it can be operated one-handed so you need not relinquish your baseball while clipping the playing field. (Courtesy, The Winterthur Library: Printed Book and Periodical Collection)

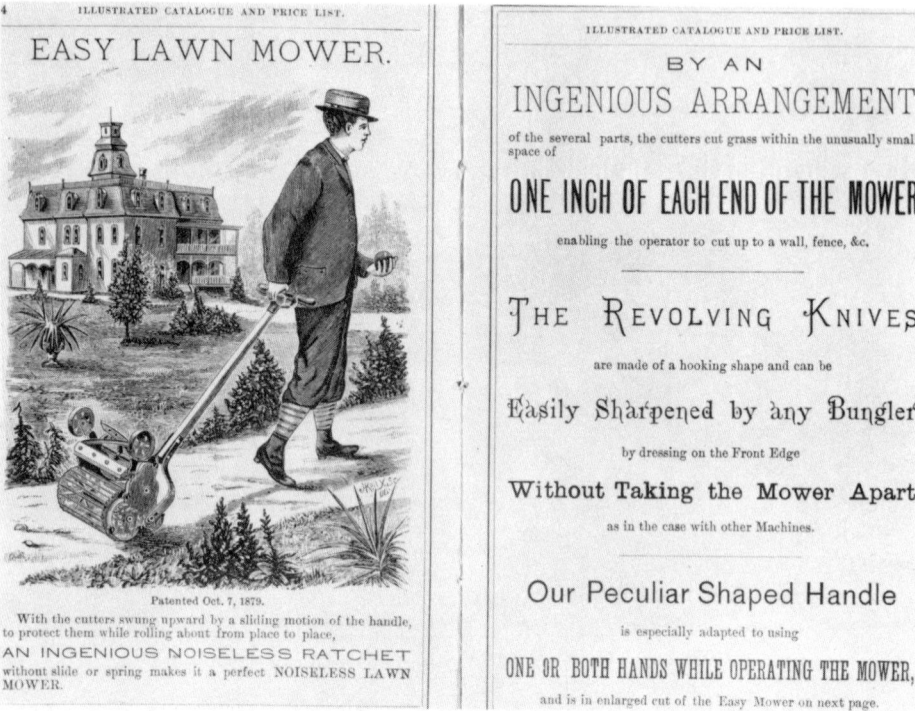

28b. 1880 catalog for Blair & Fiske's of Springfield Massachusetts. (Courtesy, The Winterthur Library: Printed Book and Periodical Collection)

The Coming of the Lawn Mower 53

A GASOLINE MOTOR LAWN MOWER.

29. It is quite astonishing to find the first gasoline-powered riding mower in use in 1897. (Scientific American, November 13, 1897)

54 Front Yard America

30. This steam-powered mower was developed by Coldwell (who built the first American mower in 1856) in 1903 for the re-classicized United States Capitol Mall. The Mall had grown into a gothic forest under Downingesque influences. The City Beautiful Movement, of which this was part, unwittingly promoted lawn mowers.

The Coming of the Lawn Mower 55

31. As this advertisement shows, the early power mowers were intended for cemeteries, parks and large estates.

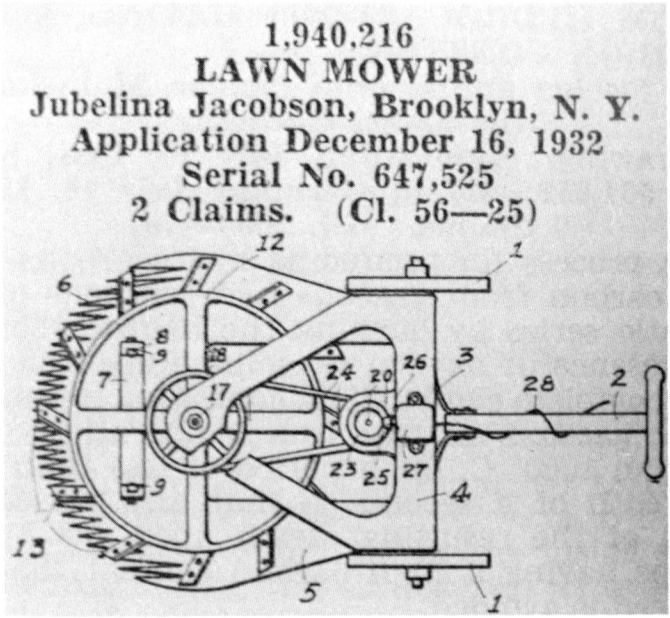

32. Jubelina Jacobson's 1933 patent is the first of the rotary blade design. The grass is held in a comb ("semi-circular series of acute-angled fingers" in Patentese) and cut by a "plurality of knives." There is no evidence that this went into production.

The Coming of the Lawn Mower 57

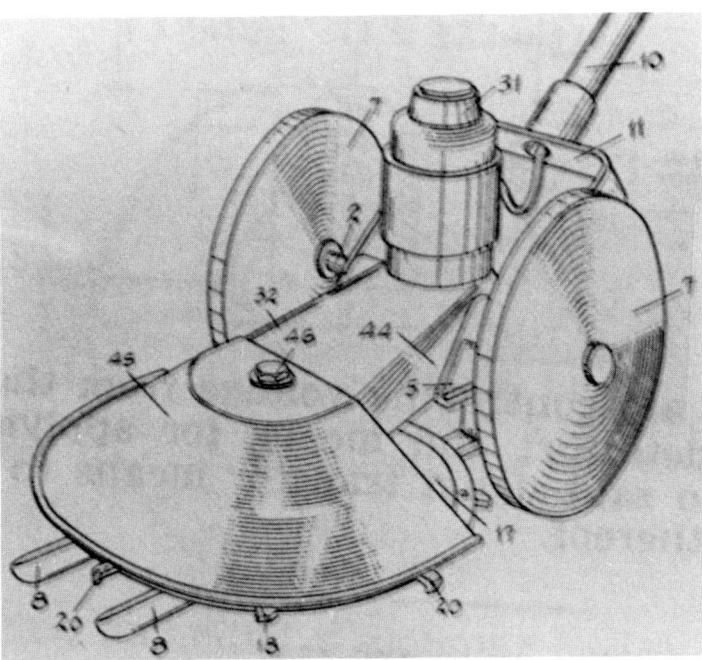

33. Bertis Urschel of Bowling Green, Ohio also has a design with cutting teeth attached to a rotating disc. Illustrated with an electric motor, the patent description mentions an internal combustion engine.

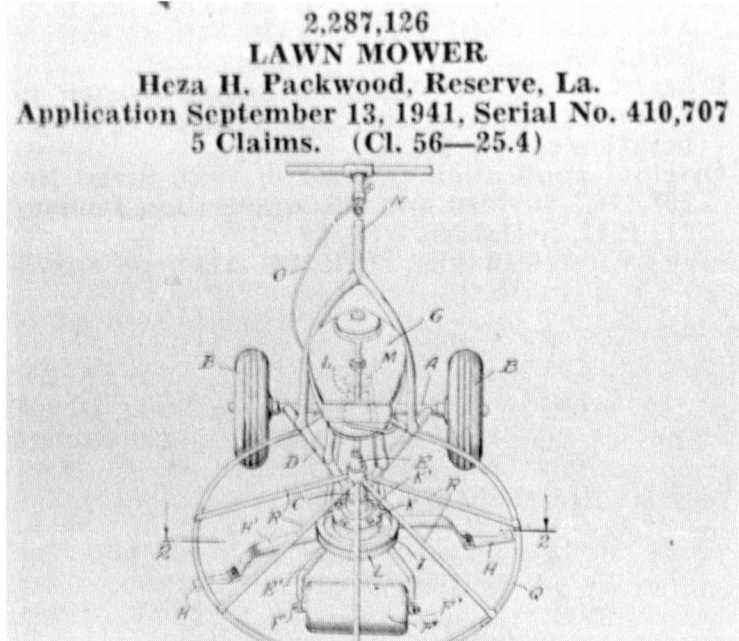

2,287,126
LAWN MOWER
Heza H. Packwood, Reserve, La.
Application September 13, 1941, Serial No. 410,707
5 Claims. (Cl. 56—25.4)

34. Heza Packwood of Reserve, Louisiana contributed two important innovations, a single rotating blade and a front roller to keep the cutter level.

The Coming of the Lawn Mower

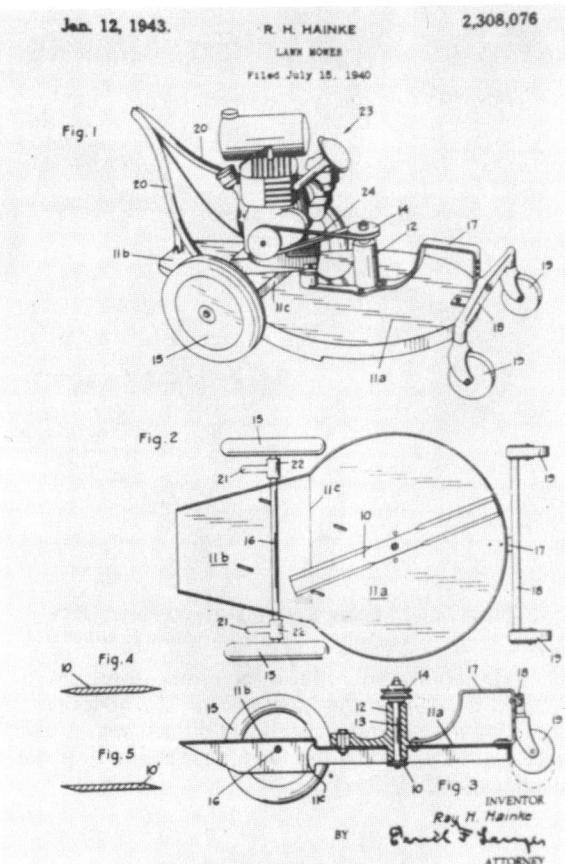

35. R.H. Hainke enclosed the blade, put four wheels on, and showed a gasoline engine. This is the prototype of the power mowers that banished reel-type hand mowers to the dump in the 1950s.

36. Extensively advertised for direct-from-factory sales in the 1940s, the Montamower did not prevail. The light weight and ability to trim flush with a wall were overbalanced by the tendency to jam. (Popular Mechanics, April 1947)

The Coming of the Lawn Mower

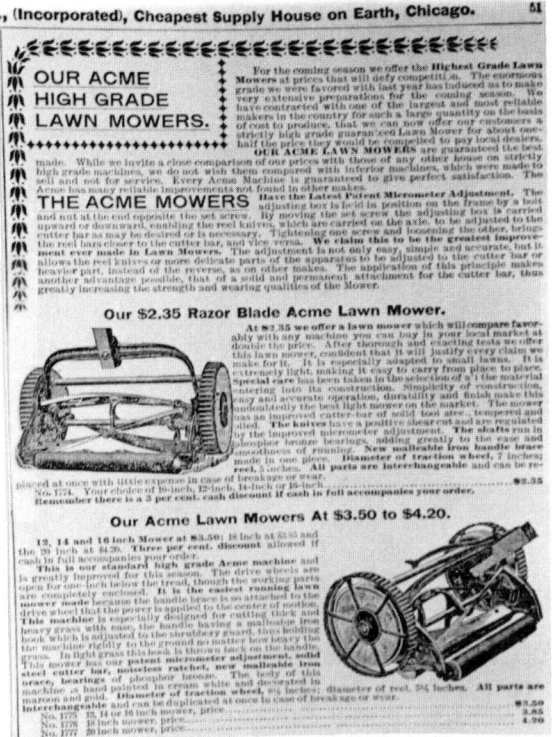

37. By 1897, the price of mowers from Sears, Roebuck put them into the reach of almost everyone, and the 14-inch mowers suited to children and ladies was giving way to wider models. By comparison, in 1993 Sears push reel mowers cut 16-18-inch swath ($69.99-$174.99). Most rotary power mowers cut 22 inches, while riding mowers clip 38-44 inch-wide strips.

The stumbling block in innovation was adherence to the idea that a lawn should be rolled, so almost all the inventions prior to 1870 are encumbered by the incorporation of large, heavy lawn rollers (e.g. patent #83,101). Rollers, of course, have the function of flattening the ground, and so are still used on new lawns and on specialized lawns for sports such as lawn tennis, croquet, putting and bowling greens, etc. But the insistence on rolling by horticulturists such as Loudon and Downing probably also relates to the unevenness of hand-scythed stubble, i.e., the roller flattened the grass. In 1870—a peak year for lawn mower patents—five inventions had a reel and roller, three were reciprocating tooth mowers, and three were light-weight reel models. There were bugs to be worked out, however. Some models had exposed gears connecting the driving wheels to the cutting reel, and these quickly jammed with grass. The solution was an enclosed journal box. Most were difficult to sharpen, until the "Philadelphia Mower" (first patented in 1869, #87,286) developed a "self-sharpening" mower that had set-screws on the "wiper" bar so that as the cutters wore, the operator could reset the wiper to a close fit. Significantly, this was the first hand-mower that *Scientific American* recommended and illustrated (20 Apr. 1878: 249), although they had acknowledged the existence of mowers as early as April 1, 1876, cautioning owners not to set them too low.

In 1879, *Scientific American* reported on an "Improved Lawn Mower" (the "Pennsylvania," by another manufacturer) which addressed another problem, the slowing of the cutting reel when cornering: "The wheels are connected with the shaft by means of a ratchet, so that the speed of the cutter is always governed by that of the wheel making the greater number of revolutions" (5 Apr. 1879: 211). By 1880, the magazine felt ready to entitle an article "Lawn Mowing Made a Pleasure," although the specific mower design that prompted the article soon disappeared (4 Sept. 1880: 146). But, by 1880, the one-person hand-mower had been perfected, and prices were bringing them within easy reach: an 1870 "Archimedes" 14" mower had cost $65; an 1872 "Philadelphia" 14" was $20; an 1888 "Henderson" 14" was $10.25; an 1897 "Acme" from the Sears, Roebuck catalog was only $3.50 in a choice of 12", 14" or 16" widths.

Manufacturers such as Coldwell produced many models including mower-roller combinations; this was, after all, the heyday of croquet and lawn tennis. Large horsedrawn mowers for estates, parks and government grounds cut up to a 40" swath. The English tended to stay with heavy mowers; it is interesting to note that the Manchester firm of Follows & Bate introduced in 1873 a light-weight *"Anglo-American"* line (Coldwell; Peter Henderson & Co.; Follows and Bate). Other power sources followed; in 1897 Thomas Coldwell (who you will recall made the first American mower circa 1855) invented a gasoline engine propelled riding mower, and in 1904 a steam mower which moved and rolled a polo field in eight hours. A "Novel Automobile Lawn Mower" reported in *Scientific American* in 1903 spelled out the advantages over the two horse-drawn machines it replaced. Horses cannot cut close to edges, need large areas for turns and their hooves dig up the turf (*Scientific American* 13 Nov. 1897: 314; 13 June 1903: 446; 30 Jan. 1904: 87). (Peter Henderson & Company sold "Horse Boots, to prevent horses from sinking in damp or soft ground" to go with their mowers.) This "Novel Automobile" 15-horsepower mower weighed a full ton and was used on the U.S. Capitol grounds. (Significantly, 1903 was the year that the implementation of the senate's plan to convert the Mall from a forest to a lawn was begun.) From this time on, motorized mowers were available, but very expensive.

An advertisement in *The Independent* in 1918 for the Fuller & Johnson Motor Lawn Mower, "Fast replacing hand mowers, horse mowers and the heavier types of motor mowers" had a price tag of $275. Another advertisement in the same magazine was for a horsedrawn "Townsend Triplex" capable of cutting a swath of over seven feet (4 May 1918 222, 224).[23] Power mowers were clearly beyond the means of the vernacular homeowner. Between the world wars a few patents were issued for smaller power mowers (#1677377, 1929337, 2041654), but most interesting were two designs for electrically motorized reel mowers. One (#1637603, patented 1927) used a worm gear to turn the cutters and a belt to drive the wheels; another (#1812272, patented 1933) incorporated the motor into the axle of the cutter. It is doubtful either went into production—the awkwardness and potential danger of a power cord continues to limit the popularity of electric mowers—but by 1940, gas-powered reel mowers were available at $69.50 (*House Beautiful* ad. 1 Apr. 1940), and both *Popular Science* (Sept. 1937: 91) and *Popular Mechanics* (Sept. 1938: 473-74) had articles on how to "Motorize Your Lawn Mower."

World War II stopped all production (the only lawn mower articles listed in the *Readers Guide* were on how to sharpen a worn mower), and even as late as the summer of 1947, *Consumer Research Bulletin* could only provide a "preliminary report" on power mowers, because the supply was "very short." This article also has the first mention of the "rotary flat-knife" type which they said was easy to push, very dangerous, and greatly overpriced (July 1947: 5-8). And, we might add, it was the first innovation in cutter design since the 1870s when the spiral reel had been refined to become the standard for all lawn mowers. In 1949, both *Consumers Research Bulletin* and *Consumer Reports* reported on a variety of home mowers, mostly reel-type, but including also the Jari sickle-bar, a motorized version of the reciprocating knives of the 1860s and agricultural harvesters (these models are popular for highway and parks departments because they will cut tall grass and shrubs); and the much advertised hand-powered Monta Mower. Weighing only 8 1/4 pounds, priced at only $22.50, "as modern and efficient as your electric razor," the Monta Mower had nine small cutters whose rotation came from equally small wheels, and, without the large driving wheels that flanked the cutting reel of the conventional mower, the Monta Mower could cut right up against walls, fences and sidewalks. Unfortunately, *Consumers Research Bulletin* could not recommend it, and in another test five years later (1954) they still found that it jammed with grass and was nowhere near equal to the reel hand mower.[24]

The innovation that would prevail, however, was the "rotary flat knife." The revolutionary concept was to spin knives parallel to the ground. The earliest patent (#1,940,216, December 19, 1933, by Jubelina Jacobson) was somewhat like a Norelco razor; the grassblades were held in a comb while a multi-bladed disc sheared them off. A 1941 patent (#2253452) retained the disc but omitted the comb. A year later a design was patented replacing the disc with a propeller-like double-blade (#2,287,126), and on January 12, 1943, Ray H. Hainke of Kensington, Kansas, patented the design from which all subsequent rotary blade mowers seem to derive (#2,308,076), whether powered by gasoline motor or electricity, pushed by hand or self-propelled, walked or ridden by the operator. Never as smooth-cutting as a well-maintained reel mower (still preferred for sports fields), rotary blade mowers are terribly dangerous for hurling projectiles at 100 mph and cutting the operator's slipping feet. Disturbers of neighborhood peace, these mowers greatly speeded the chore of grass-mowing. They will level the sward even when the knives are as dull as the side of a screwdriver, and suitably abused, they will convert any meadow or copse, into the semblance of a lawn. These motorized rotary mowers became the standard by 1960, enlarged rural lawns and invited owners of acre-plus lots to emulate Capability Brown and A.J. Downing with picturesque dells, bosky paths and curving borders. They also came onto the market as the G.I. Bill of Rights guaranteed the American Dream of a house in the subdivision to hundreds of thousands of families. And they satisfied deep needs in the American male. Prior to these mowers, domestic mechanically powered necessaries were in the woman's domain: vacuum cleaners, Mixmasters, sewing machines. Nineteenth-century advertising

66 Front Yard America

featured women and children to underscore the easy operation of light-weight mowers, but mowing has always been a masculine chore, in the main. In a rather too cute feature essay in *Smithsonian*, Richard Wolkomir said that mowing is one of Man's "last gender-affirming chores, an analog for saber-toothtiger bonking." Noting that in 1989 consumers spent $5,700,000,000 on lawn care, he states that American men "mow a 31,250-square-mile lawn belt, more or less contiguous from Eastport, Maine, to Mendocino, California." In the language of emblematic T-shirts of the 1990s, the old saw that "a mother's work is never done" converts to "A Father's Lawn Work is Never Done."

38. The practice of having photo portraits taken of homes is rare before 1890, leaving the researchers dependent upon suspect lithographs in county atlases. But three authentically dated photographs from Litchfield, Connecticut show a concentrated period of transition. The Elmore House on Meadow Street was photographed in the last quarter of the nineteenth century with a substantial fence. (Litchfield Historical Society)

The Coming of the Lawn Mower 67

39. Litchfield was settled in the 1720s and remains one of the best preserved New England villages with fine homes and churches from the late eighteenth and early nineteenth centuries. The acceptance of new landscaping styles in a traditional community underscores how pervasive the changes were. The Hickox House on East Street was photographed in Spring of 1888 with a transparent pipe fence that could afford no barrier to any animals except horses and cattle. (Litchfield Historical Society)

40. One year after the Hickox photo, this view of the Bissell House shows a clipped, spreading lawn and outdoor living room space on the porch and lawn. Needless to say, not every place in Litchfield abandoned the picket fence tradition. (Litchfield Historical Society)

The Coming of the Lawn Mower 69

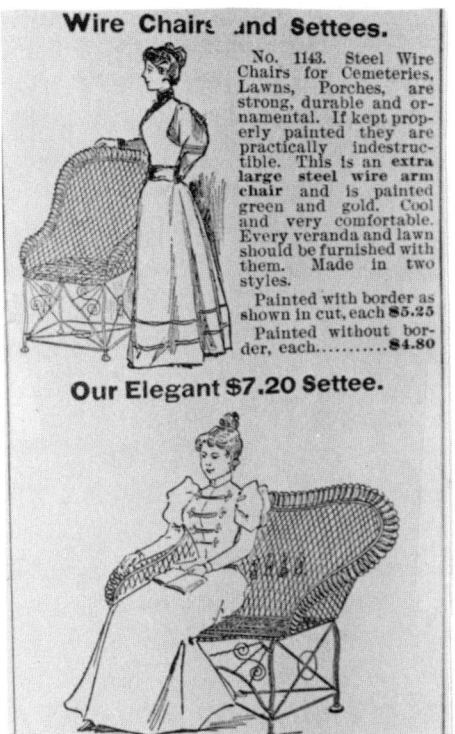

41. Early photographs show regular indoor furniture being used outdoors. With neatly clipped lawns, outdoor furniture and yard equipment start to be a major industry. The 1897 Sears Roebuck catalog has lawn furniture, tents, croquet sets and tennis outfits.

70 Front Yard America

42. How dramatic the revolution in home landscaping was can be seen in these two sets of contrasting views. In 1886, Andrew Morrison depicted an elegant St. Paul neighborhood dominated by iron fences. (Minnesota Historical Society)

43. Fourteen years later, the new up-cult neighborhood was a fenceless Summit Avenue. (Haas & Wright photo, Minnesota Historical Society)

The Coming of the Lawn Mower

44. Two contemporaneous photographs of Springfield, Illinois. The first is the front yard of the Gehrmann Place. The brick mansion was in the middle of a city block of exotic landscaping. The walks are gravelled; the grass (lower right) is scythed in the old-fashioned way advocated by A.J. Downing. The garden was laid out in the early 1870s; this view was in 1900. (Guy Mathis Collection, Illinois State Historical Library)

72 Front Yard America

45. True egalitarianism obtains in the fenceless yards connecting the corner residence of Isaac Ransom with those of his tenants. A lawnmower has been at work in this 1900 view. (Illinois State Historical Library)

The Coming of the Lawn Mower

46. In this circa 1910 photograph, a lawn mower has been the only means of separating the wild prairie from the outdoor living room. A "conversation area" of two homemade chairs and a park bench is on the left; a glide hangs on the porch. (Minnesota Historical Society)

Part Five

Developing an Aesthetic for the Democratic Front Yard

The underlying aesthetic for the American front yard was firmly established in the eighteenth century. It is the very elite English landscape garden tradition, exemplified by Lancelot "Capability" Brown's grounds at Blenheim Palace near Oxford. On this large scale its influence can be felt everywhere, and like Blenheim, generally not for exclusiveness but for public pleasure and political show. Even such baroque grounds as Chatsworth, Versailles and Pierre L'Enfant's eighteenth-century design for the United States capitol mall owed their predominant geometrical forms at least in part to the English picturesque tradition, best characterized by Alexander Pope's happy phrase "nature methodized." Cemeteries in this style, designed as much to be retreats for the urban living as well as for the dead, began in Paris in 1804 with Pere Lachaise and in America in 1831 at Mt. Auburn in Cambridge, Massachusetts. The "rural cemetery" soon became the preferred form in cities large and small. In the heart of New York City, Woodlawn Cemetery today has picturesque vistas to equal those at Chatsworth, Stowe or Stourhead (Bergman 15, 17). With the design for New York City's Central Park in 1858 by Calvert Vaux and Frederick Law Olmsted, the English aesthetic became the model for public parks;[25] and around 1890, golf links embodied the tradition of nature picturesquely methodized (Bergman 12). One can argue with some justification that much of the U.S. Interstate Highway System is like a Blenheim at 60 mph. But none of this scales down to the 25- to 50-foot lot, which, it must be remembered, is our defined topic.

The English landscape-garden was undoubtedly "Americanized" by A.J. Downing—Americanized in climate, cultivars and scenery, first of all, but Americanized also in the egalitarian tenor of his arguments. A few passages from a June 1852 essay on "American vs. British Horticulture" will demonstrate this sort of Americanization:

But taking it for granted that our gardeners are wholly foreigners, and mostly British, they all have the disadvantage of coming to us, even the best educated of them, with their practice wholly *founded upon a climate the very opposite ours*.... [I]n fact, no two languages can be more different than the gardening tongues of England and America. The ugly words of English gardening are *damp, wet, want of sunshine, canker*. Our bugbears are *drought, hot sunshine, great stimulus to growth, and blights and diseases resulting from sudden checks*.... For theorists, who know little of human nature, it is easy to answer—"well, when British gardeners come to a climate totally different from their own...why, they will open their eyes to such glaring facts, and alter their practice accordingly." Very good reasoning indeed. But anyone who knows the effect of habit and education on character, knows that it is as difficult for an Irishman to make due allowance for American sunshine and heat, as for a German to forget sour-kraut [sic], or a Yankee to feel an instinctive reverence for royalty. (*Rural Essays* 84-85)

There is also democratization in Downing's writings and cottage plans in the general scaling down, not only from ducal estates like Castle Howard or Chatsworth, but with examples of a very modest size—"starters," so to speak, in the parlance of realtors of the 1970s and 1980s. Nevertheless, Downing is speaking of "country seats," not farmhouses *per se*, nor the mass-market suburban developments that begin to appear in the 1870s. The suburbs of the early years had expansive lots—one to twenty acres in the first American "villa park" Llewellyn Park, New Jersey, begun during the Civil War years (Stilgoe, *Borderland* 52-55). But for our purposes, it is worth quoting Downing on the subject of fences in his 1841 *A Treatise on the Theory and Practice of Landscape Gardening adapted to North America with a view to the Improvement of Country Residences*:

Fences are often the most unsightly and offensive objects in country seats...the close proximity of fences to the house gives the whole place a confined and mean character.... Nothing is more common in the places of cockneys who become inhabitants of the country ["cockney" is Downing's term for urban ex-patriates given to ostentatious over-building and ornamentation, see *Rural Essays* 224-228] than to display immediately around the dwelling a spruce paling of carpentry, neatly made, and painted white or green; an abomination among the fresh fields, of which no person of taste could be guilty.... (272-273)

This passage requires some interpretation in the context of the time and in the context of Downing's other writing. The year, 1841, is five years before Downing was to write that there were no fine lawns in America and before Downing had traveled to England where he may have seen Budding's lawn mower. Almost a decade after 1841, Downing still could complain about the prevalence of free-roaming livestock (his town of Newburgh being the "only one among all the towns, cities and villages of New York, where pigs and geese have not the freedom of the streets" [*Rural Essays* 238]). At the same time (1850), he notes for the first time *plans* for suburban developments that he views both skeptically and in scornful tone, stating:

Well, the beau-ideal of these newly-planned villages is not down to the zero of dirty lanes and shadeless roadsides; but it rises, we are sorry to say, no higher than the streets, lined on each side with shade-trees, and bordered with rows of houses...built on fifty-foot lots... (240)

While this may seem to belabor the point, its significance will appear shortly. But it is certainly clear that Downing does not *oppose* fences, that his objection is to fences built close around rural dwellings that are in expansive settings and that he, like virtually all landscape architects after, disdains small-lot commissions.

Thus, we see that Capability Brown, Humphrey Repton and others set the aesthetic for "yards" in aristocratic England, and Andrew Jackson Downing Americanized the aesthetic. The *democratizer* of the aesthetic, however, was Frank Jesup

Scott of Toledo, Ohio. Parts of his biography are elusive, and the problem of how his aesthetic became the predominant vernacular style for owner-occupied single family residences in America and Canada must remain speculative, but the direct link to Downing is unquestionable. Scott's father was a Yankee land speculator, an enthusiastic booster of Northwest Ohio as an early editor of the Toledo *Blade* newspaper, and a philanthropist who donated the land for what became the University of Toledo. Jesup Scott's son, Francis, was born in 1828 in South Carolina from where he migrated with his family to Ohio in 1830. In an early boom, the father sold land in the amount of $400,000. Most was lost in a panic, but by the mid-1840s he had recouped, owning almost all the downtown property of Toledo. From then on, the Scotts' family fortunes were more than secure, and it seems clear that precocious young Frank's whimsies were well-supported.

In 1846, at age 18, Frank Scott came into possession of A.J. Downing's *Treatise on the Theory and Practice of Landscape Gardening*, and for some five years studied landscape gardening, spending one summer with Downing at Newburgh and another summer with Downing and Calvert Vaux, the English architect known later for his collaborative work with Frederick Law Olmsted on Central and Riverside Park in New York City, Prospect Park in Brooklyn, and, in 1868-69, the highly influential plan for the Chicago suburb of Riverside, Illinois. As Vaux did not emigrate to America until 1850 and Downing's tragic and heroic death occurred in the summer of 1852, (he helped passengers to escape a burning riverboat), it seems probable that Scott's association with Downing was in the late forties and with Vaux in 1851. In 1853 and 1854 he was in Europe, presumably studying architecture, as he had abandoned the dream of being a landscape architect because of the "poverty of the country" in "swamp-and-sand-hill Toledo." On his return from Europe he may have opened an architectural office in Toledo, though in the flyleaf of the Downing volume that he later gave to his city's library, he says "I was verdant enough to open an office in Toledo in the Autumn of 1857, when the chances were less hopeful than they are today in Alaska." (The Downing first edition was donated to the Toledo library in 1904.) In 1857 he did design a house, a large Italianate dwelling with square towers that one source suggests was the first of this kind. But that seems to have been both beginning and end of his career as a practicing architect. In 1859, he traveled to South America, and in 1860 (the dates are muddy) he had a shipboard wedding to Anna Marie Walsh "a lady he had known in Paris" off the coast of Takahuano, Chile. A curtain now draws across his youthful careers; sometime there was a divorce (one imagines immediately) and in 1859 (60?) Frank Jesup Scott joined his father and brothers Maurice and William in the real estate business.[26]

Ten years later Scott publishes what is very likely the only book that actually *advocates* as a positive aesthetic contiguous, unfenced front yards joining together modest-sized rectangular lots along straight streets. This book, *The Art of Beautifying Suburban Home Grounds of Small Extent; the Advantages of Suburban Homes over City and Country Homes, The Comfort and Economy of Neighboring Improvements; The Choice and Treatment of Building Sites; and the Best Modes of Laying Out, Planting and Keeping Decorated Grounds* is recorded in editions of 1870, 1872, 1873, 1883 and 1886, which certainly points toward popularity and probably toward some degree of influentiality, though nothing to be compared to Downing's.

Before setting forth Scott's aesthetic ideas and rationales, however, we should emphasize the significance of his departures from the dictates of his mentors, Andrew Jackson Downing and Calvert Vaux. The first is lot size and shape. Even though most of Scott's plans are for good-sized residences, he insists in italics that *"From a half acre to four or five acres will afford ground enough to give all the fine pleasures of rural life"* (29), while the designs that make him a trendsetter and revolutionary are for lots 50 x 150, more in the nature of one-sixth acre (Plate XXII 214). Downing had deplored such small-scaled plans. The passage by Downing quoted above about 50-foot lots continues: "if any buyer is not satisfied with that amount of elbow room, he may buy two lots, though certain that his neighbor will still be within twenty feet of his fence" and further, the suburban village design "should aim at something higher than mere rows of houses upon streets crossing each other at right angles, and bordered with shade-trees" (*Rural Essays* 240). We will return to this passage, but suffice it to say that Scott's advocacy of small lots on a grid of straight streets is not "proper." When the firm of Olmsted and Vaux wrote their plan for Riverside, Illinois in 1868, they did provide for 50-foot lots (though preferring 100-foot frontages which the 1869 developers' "Prospectus" was actually to maintain as the minimum standard), but they decidedly eschewed "the constantly repeated right angles, straight lines and flat surfaces which characterize our large modern towns" ("Riverside, Illinois" 280, 287, 274).

What is the significance of these major departures from the guidance of Downing and Vaux and the legacy of Capability Brown? Simply that Frank J. Scott is an American real estate man in the business of designing salable property, not that of landscaping property belonging to millionaires. Described as "one of the very shrewdest real estate men in the city," he was himself a millionaire who "owned more frontage of down-town property than any individual in Toledo" (Scott Papers). And this statement is made some half-dozen years after he had retired to life on the French Riviera with a second wife whom he had married in 1893 when he was 65.

Shrewd in real estate, Scott was equally shrewd in his *Art of Beautifying Suburban Home Grounds*, for in it, practical social analysis and aesthetics join hands to a degree that is possibly unprecedented and rare since. Unlike other landscape and house architects, Scott can be disinterested in his aesthetics, because he had given up looking for clients more than a decade before.

Developing an Aesthetic 83

The first thing he does is to dispense with all the romantic claptrap about the joys of rural life. We're talking about suburbs and "the man who must leave his home after an early breakfast to attend to his office or store business, and who only returns to dinner and tea.... Tired with town labor his home must be to him a haven of repose," rather than a place for the double labor of horticultural digging, pruning and weeding, or the added expense of gardener's bills. No, "A velvety lawn, flecked with sunlight and the shadows of common trees, is very inexpensive, and may be a very elegant refreshment for the business-wearied eye." Without a strong desire and an education for floral gardening *the art of making pictures with trees, lawn and flowers*...it is best that the more elegant forms of gardening art should be dispensed with, and only simple effects attempted...a well-kept lawn alone produces that kind of beauty..." along with "large trees...to enliven their beauty" (23). So much for the weary businessman's needs. How about his wife and family? Here is where Scott argues in favor of suburban *lots* as opposed to suburban *parks*, and here we must allow him to speak at length, for he introduces women's lives, values and concerns into *community design* for the first time, as the year before, Catherine Beecher and Harriet Beecher Stowe had introduced feminism into *home design* in their 1869 *The American Woman s Home; or Domestic Science.* Scott says:

A serious inconvenience of extensive private grounds, or parks is the isolation and loneliness of the habitual inmates of the house—the ladies. Few, even of those who have a native love for rural life, can long live contented without pleasant near neighbors. A large family may feel this less than a small one. Those who have the means, the health, and the disposition to entertain much company at home, will escape the feeling of loneliness. But much company brings much care. It is paying a high price for company when one must keep a free hotel to secure it. To do without it, however, soon suggests to the ladies that fewer acres, and more friends near by, would be a desirable change; and not knowing the facility with which the happy medium may be reached, they are apt to jump at the conclusion that, of the two privations—life in the country without neighborly society, or life in the city without the charms of Nature—the latter is the least. Thousands of beautiful homes are every year offered for sale, on which the owners have often crippled their fortunes by covering too much ground with their expenditures. Instead of retiring to the country for rest and strengthening recreation, they have added a full assortment of losing and vexatious employments in the country to their already wearisome but profitable business in the city. It is the ambition to have "parks" (young Chatsworths!)—to be model farmers and famous gardeners; to be pomologists, with all the fruits of the nursery catalogues on their lists: in short, to add to the burden of their town business the cares of half a dozen other laborious professions, that finally sickens so many of their country places after a few years' experience with them. There is another large class of prosperous city men who have spent their early years on farms, and who cherish a deep love of the country through all their decennial rounds of city life; who have no fanciful ambitions for parks; whose dreams are of hospitable halls, broad pastures, and sweet meadows, fine cattle and horses. It is a less vexatious mesh of ambitions than the preceding, but one that requires a very thoughtful examination of the resources of the purse and the calls that will be made upon it, before purchasing the model farm that is to be. And we beg leave to intrude a little into the privacy of the family circle, to inquire how long will the wife and daughters be content with isolation on ever so beautiful a farm; how long before the boys will leave home for business or home of their own; and how long, if these are dissatisfied, or absent, will the "fine mansion" and broad fields, in a lonely locality, bring peace and comfort to the owner? That there are men and families that truly fill, enjoy, and honor such life, it is good to know; but they are cluster-jewels of great rarity.

Our panacea for the town-sick business man who longs for a rural home, whether from ennui of the monotony of business life, or from the higher nature-loving soul that is in him, is to take country life as a famished man should take food—in very small quantities. (27-29)

The "small quantities" are not only justified for social values, but financially, too. As the technology of the hand lawn mower was making "velvety lawns" possible, so it was various other technologies that were making suburbs possible—"horse and steam railways and steamers"—but Scott insists that additional technological amenities of *urban* life must be incorporated:

...if we are to choose a suburban residence for the whole year (not migrating to a city home or hotel with the first chills of November), it is a serious matter to know whether there is a good hard road and sidewalk to the home. City life, with its flagging [sidewalks, etc.], and gas lights, and pavements, comes back to the imagination *couleur de rose* when your horses or your boots are toiling through deep mud on country roads. This is bad enough by daylight; at night you might feel like stopping to bestow a benediction on a post that would sparkle gas-light across your path. Now the moral which we would suggest by thus presenting the most disagreeable feature of suburban life, is this: to go no farther into the country than where good roads have already been made, and where good sidewalks have either been made, or, from the character or growth of the neighborhood, are pretty sure to be made within a short time. One of the greatest drawbacks to the improvement of suburban neighborhoods is the fact that many persons own long fronts on the roads who are not able to make the thorough improvement of roads and sidewalks in front of their grounds which the new-comers, located beyond them, require. This should have been foreseen by the new-comers. Having chosen their homes with the facts before them, they must not complain if some poor farmer or "land-poor" proprietor is unable to improve for their benefit, and unwilling to sell at their desire. In choosing a suburban home, the character of the ownerships between a proposed location and the main street or railroad station should be known, and influence to some extent one's choice.

Once more, we hear the voice of the commercial developer rather than an *artiste*. Scott's proposal is for "companies of congenial gentlemen" to buy land enough for all, divide it into "deep narrow strips, if the form of the ground will admit of it, having frontages of one, two or three hundred feet each, according to the means respectively of the partitioners.... Acting together, the little community can create a local pressure for good improvements that will have its effect on the entire street and neighborhood" (29-30).

The "congenial company" approach is undoubtedly modeled on the Riverside Improvement Company. Not only was Scott a friend of Vaux, but the Olmsted & Vaux report on Riverside dwells upon access from Chicago, drainage, street paving quite as much as creating an "inhabited park" ("Riverside, Illinois" 285). The term "park," though, Scott wants banished from the American vocabulary except for public parks and cemeteries:

Parks of considerable extent, as private property, are impracticable, by reason of the transient nature of family wealth, in a republic where both the laws and the industrial customs favor rapid divisions and new distributions. Attempts to make and keep great private parks are generally conspicuous failures. Some of the old family parks on the Hudson River, and a few in other parts of the country, may be thought of as exceptions, but they are exceptions which rather prove the rule; for most of them are on portions of manorial grants, held under almost feudal titles, which have remained in the same families through several generations, simply because they are held under laws which present a jarring contrast with the general laws of property which now govern in most of the States. It would be well for our progress in Landscape Gardening that this word park, as applied to private grounds, should be struck out of use, and that those parts of our grounds which are devoted to what feeds the eye and the heart, rather than the stomach, should be called simply HOME-GROUNDS; and that the ambition of private wealth in our republic should be to make gems of home beauty on a small scale, rather than fine examples of failures on a large scale. (26-27)

Developing an Aesthetic 87

Scott's scheme for making "gems of home beauty on a small scale" is set forth in a drawing and description in the last part of his book where he commends layouts and plantings for a variety of suburban homes. In Plate XXII, however, he has five modest homes in a block with 250 feet of frontage and a depth of 150 feet. Each has a 50 x 50 back plot for fruit trees and vegetables.

The houses themselves are such as proprietors often build in rows for the purpose of adding to the value, and increasing the sale of adjacent property; but the connection of all the fronts into one long lawn is yet seldom practiced. The elegant effect, however, which this mode of improvement lends to places which, without it, were small and cheap-looking, will add thousands of dollars to their saleable value. It gives a genteel air to the neighborhood that five times the expenditure in buildings would fail to produce, and serves by this fact alone to attract a class of refined people of small means, who might not find the common run of houses, of the cost of these, sufficiently attractive to induce them to select homes....

The essential feature of the planting on this neighborhood plan is this: that *back of a line ten or twelve feet from the front street, to the foot-step of the porches, there shall be no shrub or tree planted on any of the fronts; and only those species of flowers which do not exceed six to nine inches in height. This secures a belt of lawn varying from fifteen to forty feet in width, the entire length of the block, and leaves ample space on each lot for a good selection and arrangement of shrubs and flowers. The light dotted lines on the plan show the leading ranges of view over this common lawn. Of course only the lightest of wire fences are to be used between the lots, if any such divisions are required; and none at all ought to be necessary.*

Lot 1 is entered from the side-street, under a gateway arbor. From this entrance the whole length of the block to B and E, two hundred and fifty feet, is a lawn, broken only by beds for low flowers, margined one side by the choicest groups of shrubbery, and on the other by the various architectural features of the steps, vases, porches, and verandas of the five houses, and their flowers and vines. Nothing can more strikingly illustrate the advantage of such neighboring improvements than the view from this point, embracing as it does, under one glance, all the beauty that may be created in the "front yards" of five distinct homes, all forming parts of a single picture. (214-217)

In all these quoted passages it is apparent that Frank J. Scott would be thoroughly in harmony with the culture of middle-class America for the next century. For one thing, population growth has shifted from rural to urban concentrations. It is a mobile society, and the sacred *home* moves from house to house. Houses, therefore, are investments in the present, not legacies to the future. As investments, outward appearance is a salable commodity. The key to salable appearance of the grounds is the same as it would become in kitchens and bathrooms: simple, neat, easy to maintain, and non-idiosyncratic. And as Scott writes in 1870 the technology is at hand to provide a "smooth, closely shaven surface of grass"; "the admirable little hand mowing machines...are now so simplified and cheapened that they are coming into general use on small pleasure grounds, and proprietors may have the pleasure of doing their own mowing without the wearisome bending of the back, incident to the use of the scythe. Whoever spends the early hours of one summer, while the dew spangles the grass, in pushing these grass-cutters over a velvety lawn, breathing the fresh sweetness of the morning air and the perfume of new mown hay, will never rest contented again in the city" (107, 110-111).

Developing an Aesthetic 89

47. In 1874 Theophilus P. Brown of Toledo published an illuminating before and after birdseye view of what may be the first "working-men's suburb." (All views courtesy Toledo-Lucas County Public Library)

90 Front Yard America

48. The "before" view of 1870 (obviously drawn after the fact) shows a duck hunter's Eden of wetlands.

49. But the commercial key to Brown's Addition was the junction of three railroads. This area was destined for industrial development. All that was needed was homes to attract factory laborers.

Developing an Aesthetic 91

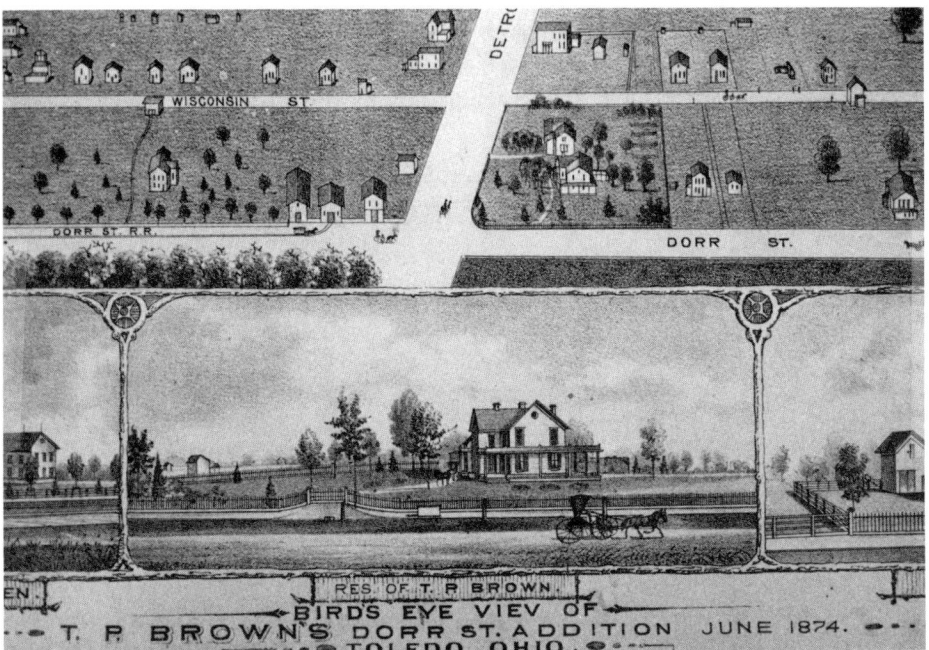

50. Brown clear-cut the woods, drained the land, subdivided it into small, affordable lots, and provided a horse street railway for easy access to downtown Toledo. By 1874 a roundhouse and factories manufacturing chairs and carriages were nearby. Neither of these views is trustworthy in details, but the commercial purposes are. Toledo's population doubled during this four-year period.

92 Front Yard America

51. Brown's Addition today. Because it was a workingmen's streetcar suburb decades before the automobile, there are no driveways to interrupt the connected yards.

52. Frank Jesup Scott, another Toledo real estate developer platted a similar workingmen's suburb called Auburndale in 1874. Scott had published the aesthetic declaration for connected yards in 1870.

Developing an Aesthetic 93

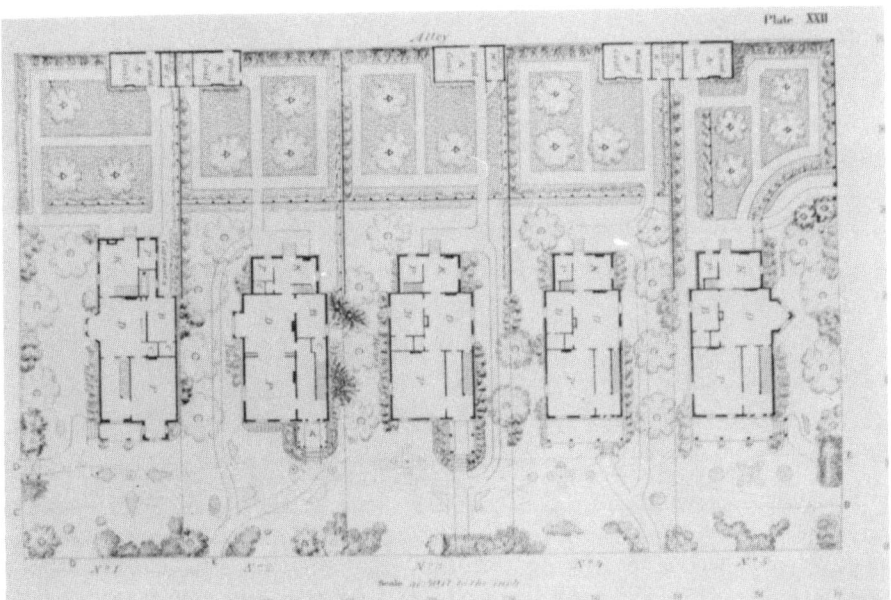

53. Scott's *The Art of Beautifying Suburban Home Grounds* had many plans for fairly extensive grounds, but in his Plate XXII he proposed a design for connected small lots fronting a straight street—the new standard for mass-marketing suburbs close to the metropolis. Notice the letter A on the porch of the second house from the left.

94 Front Yard America

54. This vignette is the projected view from porch A. With contiguous lawns, everyone can have the vistas of the English aristocracy and A.J. Downing's rich clients. Notice that the street (right) is rendered invisible by dense woody plantings. How influential Plate XXII may have been for homeowners remains an open question.

Developing an Aesthetic 95

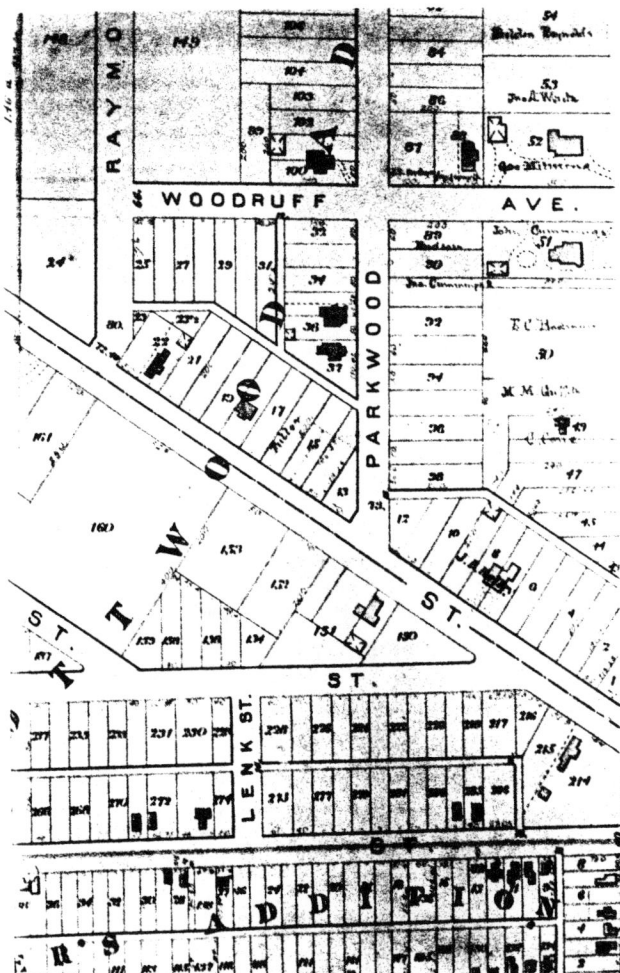

55. Scott put his aesthetic into practice in his Scottwood Addition. Lots were larger than in Brown's Addition and in Auburndale...(Toledo-Lucas County Library)

56. ...but as this 1991 view in Scottwood shows, except for those who might afford two 50-foot parcels, the spacious effect didn't work.

Part Six

To Practice as I Preach: Auburndale and Scottwood

Although A.J. Downing wrote critically in 1850 of having seen plans for suburban villages with 50-foot lots along grids of straight streets, the lots presumably set apart by fences, it is uncertain that any of these were built until after the Civil War.[27] It is certain though that the "fenceless state" does not appear until after 1870, the year of Frank Jesup Scott's *Art of Beautifying Suburban Home Grounds*. The question now is whether the American front yard actually originated in Toledo, Ohio. It is a reasonable theory, because this man who originated the social and aesthetic rationale was a member of an extremely wealthy family real estate firm in Toledo, a booming city whose population doubled in the four years 1870 to 1874 from 30,000 to 60,000. This population was accommodated through several subdivisions (or "additions") including two Scott developments, Auburndale and Scottwood, both platted in 1874 (the same year that his pioneer father died at the age of 85). These seem to have been anticipated by a year or so with the subdivision of Theophilus Brown, still known as Brown's Addition. This deserves our attention because he is an especially good example of the kind of entrepreneur who democratized the suburban movement. According to a handwritten biography in the Toledo-Lucas County Public Library, Brown settled in Toledo as a young man in 1857. In 1870[28] he purchased 160 acres of forest and swampland adjoining the juncture of three railroads, cleared it, platted 900 lots, graded streets, built some sidewalks and at a public auction sold 1/2-acre lots, (obviously each composed of three of the platted lots). He netted $50,000. Significantly, he also built a street railway to his Addition. Even more significantly, an 1874 comparative bird's-eye view shows that between the time of his purchase and the auction, a major roundhouse was built along the tracks. In short, this was a workingman's suburb, and a drive along his streets today shows that those 1/2-acre lots were soon divided into 25-foot frontages."[29] Brown's career turned to railroad speculation; along with interurban investments, he built a total of three street railways in Toledo. It is certainly easy to read between the lines and imagine that Brown knew of industrial development west of downtown Toledo, snapped up undeveloped acreage, and got in on the ground floor by providing the industrial infrastructure for what was rapidly becoming a nationwide suburban boom. The "horsecar revolution" had started in Philadelphia in 1858-1859; Chicago's first suburban horsecar railroads seem to have been in 1864. So Brown's development is in the first decade of this revolution, even anticipating the many mass-housing developments of S.E. Gross around Chicago, which followed the Great Fire of 1871, but did not hit stride until the 1880s (Stilgoe, *Borderland* 131ff; 140ff; Clark).

It may be important to note a peculiarity of Toledo's history of real estate. The city's "early projectors...were determined to get what benefits would arise from the growth of the city, and with this end in view, they not only purchased all the available property within a radius of a dozen miles, but platted the greater part of it and had it enrolled *within the city limits*. Hence, Toledo, even when it was a village of a few thousand inhabitants, covered an area which was scarcely equaled by any city in the country. There was nothing compact about it. The houses were set in large yards (they had not yet attained the *dignity of lawns*) and were *far enough apart* to give them a somewhat *isolated appearance*" (*Toledo Illustrated* 37). [Italics mine.]

Which lays the ground for Scott's "neighboring improvements," designed to counteract rural/suburban isolation and to produce a unified landscape effect along straight streets. Scott's Auburndale Addition resembles Brown's and seems also to have been aimed at working classes. Today's Auburndale shows a slightly deeper setback from the sidewalk than does Brown's Addition. Scottwood is a different matter. Platted with 50-foot lots (Toledo has major diagonal streets that force some triangular and trapezoidal departures from strict rectangular lots), a prospectus map in the *Toledo City Directory* of 1877-1878 shows that a number of multiple lots had already been claimed—the largest to M.A. Scott (about 300 x 400), a somewhat smaller lot to Frank Scott himself. The prospectus reads:

This Addition, adjoining the "Swayne Place," is now the most Central of all the newly platted parts of the City. The great depth of the lots, the fine trees upon them, the high character of the residents of the neighborhood, and its convenience to business by means of the Monroe Street Railroad [a major diagonal artery], are advantages to invite the best class of people.

Terms of Sale 1/8 down and balance in seven equal annual payments. *Interest at 6 per cent to those who will Build Speedily.*

How did these real estate developments look? Fortunately, houses with fenceless lawns became the "Art Work of Toledo" (the title of an 1895 portfolio and a 1901 sequel), while the 1888 *Toledo Illustrated* and the 1907 *City of Toledo, Ohio Through a Camera* have numerous photographs of front yard vistas. What they don't show is what one can see today: regardless of how spacious the contiguous vistas may have been, the 50-foot lots provided little space between neighbors. The majority of extant houses are variants on what Alan Gowans has named "four-square comfortable houses" (84-89). Most of the neighborhoods are well-maintained, but with mature trees, shrubs and some hedges and fences, it takes a practiced eye to see the archaeological survival of Scott's 1870 ideal, or the expansive street views that were published while the boulevard trees were maturing. Undoubtedly the highest fulfillment of Scott's landscape dream is a 1938 view of Winthrop Street, one of the many areas abutting Scottwood and only a block or so from Scott High School. With a pre-Dutch-elm disease fan-arched nave of evenly spaced trees, every house has a "foundation planting," but a communistic mower could clip merrily up and down the block hindered only by the awareness that there are strictly invisible barriers of ownership as real in their effect on neighbors' lives as the invisible Equator is on the seasons. Without question, it is a beautiful scene, and in it is one of the clearest expressions of the front yard as democratic, open, egalitarian, and a proud ornament of the neighborhood and for the community.

It is also a triumph of real estate development. The simplicity of Scott's regular rectangular plots and the economy of what was essentially an "unlandscaped" front, liberated suburban developers from the need for landscape architects and made possible attractive neighborhoods for the *mass market*, perhaps for the first time in history. It most certainly facilitated resale value as well, by eliminating idiosyncratic high-maintenance gardens and walls.

Yet the importance of Scott's work is not in Scottwood or in *The Art of Beautifying Suburban Home Grounds* so much as it is in its wholesale adaptation nationwide. How did the design invade Brown's workingman's Addition? How did it spread so widely and so thoroughly? How did it advance from a commonplace practice to an ingrained habit of perception of beauty? And how did it become one of the main visual expressions of the American character? These conundrums are the topic for the next section, but first a curious sidenote on practicing as one preaches. In the Toledo-Lucas County Public Library is a stereoscopic photo of the residence of Frank J. Scott. It is on a corner lot with a horizontal-board fence around it, and it not only lacks a sweep of lawn, but the entire lower story of the Italianate carpenter gothic house is obscured by a veritable jungle of fruit trees, shrubs and vines! The explanation of this act of landscape treason (or hypocrisy) is that this is the home of his widowed mother, and he apparently moved in with her after his father's death. In short, this was not his home nor was it in the suburbs. The photograph was probably made in 1876 when Scott was building a major residential hotel, the Hotel Madison, where, presumably as a bachelor he lived until 1893 while in Toledo. However, during those years, he also spent long summers in the Idaho Territory, mapping the Sawtooth Mountains and providing the first accurate account of the sources of rivers. But we are drifting from the subject.

Part Seven

As Toledo Goes, So Goes the Nation

Returning to the opening pages of this essay, the demonstration of precisely how a major change in cultural values and their expression takes place is a research challenge. The fact that there is a now-you-see-it-now-you-don't change in the American vernacular domestic landscape between circa 1865 and 1900 has been fairly easy to document. But there is a mysterious, elusive middle stage akin to the chrysalis stage of the metamorphosis of a caterpillar into a monarch butterfly. The caterpillar moves, has many legs, no wings; the butterfly moves, has six legs and wings and bears no resemblance to its youthful form; neither is like the chrysalis which doesn't move, but encases the caterpillar that is metamorphosing into the lovely butterfly. Very likely an entomologist can dissect a series of chrysalides and demonstrate about where one can change the name. Yet it is a question of *becoming*, not of sudden transformations like those of Ovid's myths. That is the challenge to the historian of popular culture, to pierce the chrysalis and to attempt to explain the phenomenon of becoming.

One thing that can be done now is to tighten up the time frame. In a sense, we can say that the clock starts ticking in 1870. But there is a 25-year period of upper-class windup before 1870. The wind-up includes Downing's Americanization of the English picturesque, the development of rural suburban residential parks as an ideal alternative to city life, the development of suburban mass transit, and some popularization of the Downingesque rural landscape in cemeteries and urban public parks. Lawn mowers prior to 1870 can also be relegated to the wind-up period. With 1870 we have Scott's book that effectively compromises the Downing aesthetic so that something of the suburban park design can be incorporated into mass-market real estate developments. In the early 1870s also, suburban towns were being platted with affordable small lots for industrial workers. Brown's Addition was one of the first. In 1869 the first efficient one-person lightweight mower (the "Philadelphia") had been patented.

The year 1870, therefore, is pivotal, but hardly revolutionary. Livestock still roamed; the first barbed wire fencing is produced in 1874, the same year that Scott laid out Scottwood. There were only a handful of scattered homes in Brown's Addition. Not until 1878 did *Scientific American* actually recommend a hand-mower, the "Philadelphia," and although Scott was advertising Scottwood, only 16 lots had been bought (or we might say "bought," as three of the 16 were claimed by Scott and his two brothers, doubtless to establish "the high character of the residents") and nothing had been built on these lots. The clock is ticking in the 1870s, and slowly accelerating, but it seems that we can tighten the time frame for the vernacularizations of the Scott aesthetic to 1880-1900. The 1881 *City Atlas* shows only 18 houses constructed in Scottdale, and of these there are only four sets where "neighboring improvements" are possible with adjoining yards. Nearby subdivisions (not Scott's) however, are growing rapidly with narrower lots and smaller houses. But contributory factors are on the rise: 40,000 tons of barbed wire manufactured in 1880 and 47,000 lawn mowers, with the price dropping below $20 dollars in the 1870s, down to $10.25 in 1888.

There are nagging questions though, the toughest of all being this: regardless of whether the continuous unfenced neighborhood lawn was first demonstrated in Scottwood, or even in Toledo, how did it leap from city to city? Moreover, how did it convert from planned subdivisions to a national vernacular norm? Underlying both is the constant problem for students of popular literature and social history: how much does a book influence group behavior? Where there are sales figures, very large sales figures, the questions are sometimes answered easily. Doctor Spock and Betty Crocker are two such examples. Where there are public outcries and national legislation, again, the influence is undeniable as with Harriet Beecher Stowe's *Uncle Tom s Cabin* and Rachel Carson's *Silent Spring*.

But for a book that had only five printings, even though these spanned 16 years from 1870 to 1886, and for which we've no idea how many were printed, the actual degree of influence is impossible to assess. Furthermore, as anyone knows of best sellers and bookclub selections, *buying* doesn't mean *reading*. And in the huge industry of house and garden how-to publishing, few books and magazines are read cover-to-cover; they are used selectively and as references. If we are looking for house plans, we select those within our means. For landscaping, for ideas that relate to our lots and purses. For planting, those for our climate. Add to this that although the *text* of Scott's book is strong and clear on lot size, lawns, fences and neighborhoods, only *three* out of *thirty* ground plans show the system of connecting a block of 50-foot lots, and the text for that ground-plan in all editions refers the reader to the wrong illustration of how the lawn view would appear!

On the other hand, in respect to influence, some readers are more equal than others. When a college president is impressed by a book on educational reform, the influence will be greater than if one of her assistant professors reads it; when a corporate CEO is taken with a new book on management, it is more important than if members of his sales team have read it. Indeed, in this respect a book of limited circulation may be more influential than a blockbuster.

At this point, however, I will abandon my objective persona for the first person, because this can only be speculation. The important readers of Scott's book would be men like himself, land developers. The short title of his book is *Suburban Home Grounds,* and suburbs were the hot commodity of the day in real estate. The emphasis is on grounds "of small extent," a topic that no one had addressed previously (and as I've shown, rarely later). Although there are some passages of flowery prose, in general Scott is practical and hard-headed, not only in respect to building sites and layouts, but in his dismissal of the concepts of country seats, parks, the romance of rural life and the aristocratic dream of establishing an estate to carry on from generation to generation. He speaks in the language of today's realtors (and once more, he may be the first). Recall that as he writes of the adjacent houses he says that proprietors (read "developers") "often build in rows for the purpose of adding to the value and *increasing the sale of adjacent property*" and that the "elegant effect" will add thousands of dollars to their salable value" (214-217). In addition, Scott addresses the question of commercial property: Plate XXVI is for "A Village Block of Stores and Residences, illustrating a mode of bringing Grounds back of Alleys into connection, for Decorative Purposes, with the Residences on the Village Street" (described on 224-232). Whether anyone put his ideas into practice (he proposes to make the alley a tunnel so that the long narrow lots connect to "pleasure grounds" behind), it shows that Scott is interested in commercial developments in the suburbs as well as low-maintenance, high-salability homes for the "town-sick business man." Related to this is his recognition of the need for putting in "improvements," such as well drained streets, sidewalks, and "even the luxury of gas in our suburban houses and roads is quite practicable in the mode of dividing and improving property which we have recommended..." (30).

If I am right that Scott's audience is land developers (the "congenial company"), we can also read his rationales for fenceless yards not as directed at homeowners, but as sales pitches for the real estate men. "[T]hat kind of fence," he says, with italic emphasis, *is best which is least seen, and best seen through* and "Our fences should be, to speak figuratively, *transparent.*" Acknowledging "the shameful freedom given to animals in many town and village streets" he yet argues for the transparency of iron fences and sod fences that can blend in with the lawn, allowing either for a raised bottom for the sweep of the scythe or gradual hollows "that a hand mowing machine can run upon...easily" (51-53). But it is in the chapter on "Neighboring Improvements" that he provides fodder for a behavioral revolution.

One of the most fertile sources of disagreements between families having grounds opening together, are incursions of boisterous children from one to another. Now it is suggested that children may be trained to respect and stop at a thread drawn across a lawn to represent a boundary, just as well as a stone wall....

Further, walls, fences and gates challenge boisterous boys to scale and swing.

If parents on both sides of the line do their duty in instructing the children not to trespass on contiguous lawns, less trouble will result from that cause than the bad feelings engendered by high outside boundary walls, that so often become convenient shields to hide unclean rubbish and to foster weeds. (62)

Robert Frost explored the ambivalence of the old proverb that "good fences make good neighbors." Those who hate the Scott aesthetic, such as the woman who deplored "our fenceless state" in 1909, ascribe to the view that the lack of boundaries invites trespassing, but Scott's view that board fences foster unneighborly disorder (not to mention the disputes over maintenance of party walls) was particularly borne out by the back yard reforms in Baltimore and New York in the early twentieth century.[30]

Scott's book, therefore, may indeed have influenced the revolution in front yards through real estate developers, who in some cases have hardened the practice legally with "restrictive deed covenants" that can forbid blocking the view within a given subdivision (Jordan, sec. 1-10, 11). It is also highly likely that developers were influenced by direct observation and by word of mouth. And it may simply be that platting rows of narrow lots coincided with the effective fencing out of farm animals and the cheap availability of lawn mowers. Fences are expensive. How expensive they were may surprise a modern reader. In 1879, the Kentucky Commissioner of Agriculture "deplored the vast expense of fencing fields. He said the total cost of fences in the United States was not less than $1,800,000,000, which differed but little from the value of livestock." For Kentucky alone, the environmental costs were tremendous: Commissioner W.J. Davies estimated that the *annual repair* of rail fences required the felling of ten million trees! Davies appears not to have yet heard of barbed wire, so his only remedy is to recommend laws to fence livestock rather than the fields. This practice had been recommended in 1871 in a national report by the U.S. Commissioner of Agriculture, but fencing laws generally were county acts, scattered piecemeal geographically and over the half-century after the Civil War (Harper 223-226).

I believe, though, that the conversion from an articulated aesthetic (Scott) and a practical solution for selling suburban lots (developer), to a national style is more easily explained, though equally difficult to document. First, there is the American Dream, something that Spiro Kostoff eloquently expressed in his *America By Design* television series and book (7-10, 65-68). The Dream is a free-standing, single-family home of one's own. Not everyone achieves it, and at present, it is getting less attainable, but I would agree with Kostoff, that relatively few Americans even today have the high-rise apartment or the condominium as the preferred fulfillment of a residential Dream. The exceptions are expensive Dreams for the childless—luxury pads in Manhattan or on Lake Shore Drive, condos at Malibu or Aspen—or retirement security near Hilton Head or Hazeltine.

What do American Dreamers do pending fulfillment of the Dream? Well, the first sentence of Henry David Theoreau's "Where I Lived and What I Lived For" chapter in *Walden* asserts that: "At a certain season of our life we are accustomed to consider every spot as the possible site for a house." And to Thoreau, the desire for housing is an antediluvian instinct recapitulated in every child playing "house as well as horse" (36). Very American, and yet the first important writer on architecture in modern history, Leon Battista Alberti in 1435 also ascribed the Dream-House mentality to humanity itself:

But how congenial and instinctive the desire and thought for building may be to our minds is evident—if only because you will never find anyone who is not eager to build something, as soon as he has the means to do so; nor is there anyone who, on making some discovery in the art of building, would not gladly and willingly offer and broadcast his advice for general use, as if compelled to do so by nature.... Or again, when we see some other person's building, we immediately look over and compare the individual dimensions, and to the best of our ability consider what might be taken away, added, or altered, to make it more elegant.... (4)

Although Alberti was looking at Palazzi and Thoreau was looking at packing crates, the behavior is familiar to modern Dreamers, who visit "home shows," save pages from *Better Homes and Gardens,* study Sunset how-to books, watch the progress on new house constructions, tour historic houses and model homes, and take Sunday drives through neighborhoods. Just as the mail order catalog became a Wish Book of material things for have-nots (and don't-yet-haves), so the street-car suburbs became Dream Neighborhoods for young couples saving their shekels for an easy-terms down payment on their own homes.

My idea of how the front yard innovation diffused, therefore, is that the same instruments that made middle-class suburbs possible—the streetcars and trolleys—were the instruments of popular diffusion. The "Trolley Song" from Vincente Minnelli's 1944 movie about the 1904 St. Louis World's Fair expresses the Sunday behavior neatly: "I went to lose a jolly hour on the trolley." What dwellers of boarding houses and rented flats would have seen were neat rows of spanking new houses, and proud homeowners plying their $10 mowers over green carpets of grass. Neighborly. Each house a castle for its family, each façade and yard an ornament to the community, and each block a spectacle of neighborly neatness to Sunday trolley-riders and strollers. This, then, is how Scott's plan came to be the internalized aesthetic which makes American residential areas look *American.*

It is a quiet revolution, its only sounds the pleasant whirring of the spiral blades of pushmowers. Angry voices of opposition are not heard until the revolution was complete, Frank Jesup Scott's book utterly forgotten, and the critics themselves thinking that the American vernacular front yard had always been so, as in Elizabeth Gordon's statement that "Originally, the traditional American garden was the front lawn."

Although I maintain that the *popularization* was effected just as described above, for the "working classes" and middle classes, this kind of informal observation and imitation must have been local, spurred by real estate developers' advertising in local papers. How it leap-frogged from city to city (especially if it is indeed the case that Toledo was the point of genesis) is not so easily explained by casual observation and imitation.

It is tempting to picture Scott standing before a national realtors' convention on July 4, 1876, declaring a new independence from the tyranny of walls and sending cheering subdividers throughout the nation to create the American look. Unfortunately, this picture is out of the question. For one thing, the term "realtor" was not coined until 1915. A viable national association (the National Association of Real Estate Boards) was not founded until 1908, its predecessor having lasted only 19 months in 1891 and 1892 (Davies 42-43), falling victim to the crash of 1893, with some members boarding trains for the convention in St. Paul only to receive notice that the meeting had been canceled. It is worth noting, though, that "Dominating the organization were the men from the active urban growth points of the time—Chicago, Toledo, Atlanta, Duluth." Real estate people like to visit places of market activity; indeed, their choice of St. Paul was for just that reason, having turned down an offer to host the convention by the oldest established board of real estate brokers in Baltimore (1858). Of St. Paul, "delegation after delegation rose to say, 'we think we can learn something there' " (Davies 47-49).

My interpretation of the foregoing is that although Scott's only national voice was through book publication, by 1890, at least, Toledo's subdivision developments would have had some currency, and the volumes of photographs called *Toledo*

Illustrated (1888), *The Art of Toledo* (1901), and *City of Toledo, Ohio Through a Camera* (1907)—largely views of neighborhoods, parks and public buildings—may not have been only for local parlor tables, but used for national promotion of a booming city. And there were less expensive, more popular ways of disseminating the gospel of Scottwood: picture postcards of street views of Toledo were good sellers at the turn of the century.[31]

In view of the foregoing, one can understand why the origins of the typical front lawn lie in the midwest. The various technologies matured at the same time that there was rapid industrial expansion in such cities as Toledo, Chicago, Milwaukee, St. Paul, Minneapolis and Duluth, places where there was space to develop subdivisions of single-family detached residences. Another technology not mentioned heretofore was also contributing to the mass-marketing of homes. Balloon-frame house construction (i.e., 2 x 4, 2 x 10 etc. lumber fastened with nails) developed in the three decades prior to the Civil War, but in the decades following, pre-cut and pre-packaged balloon frame houses followed pioneer cabins, soddies and shanties into rural areas. The Aladdin and Sears, Roebuck mail order pre-packaged homes soon were ready for upper-middle-class suburbs, as well as for working classes (see Gowans and F.W. Peterson). On the other hand eastern cities not only were established, but had long established traditions of rowhouses and tenements, both of which obviated front yards. In such cities as Boston and New York, space was severely limited, making the contrast with Toledo's expansive platting even more pointed. Furthermore, the suburban movement of the east more directly evolved out of Downing's rural parks. Front yards with contiguous lawns did diffuse east, but most saliently in such developments as the Greenbelt movement of the 1930s and the postwar Levittown phenomena.

It is also clear that Elizabeth Gordon's theory that legal restrictions early in the century forced the nationalization of the open-front style is in error. As to the practice of subdividers to regulate the common appearance by means of contracted restrictions, these were in 1909 "just becoming accepted procedure to preserve the character of subdivisions." A couple years later, responding to "The City Beautiful" movement, members of NAREB indulged in spirited discussions about "ordinances for building lines and set-backs, *still new and not well accepted*" (Davies 65-69, *italics mine*). What was accepted in 1909 even by one of the most innovative developers, William E. Harmon, a pioneer in installment selling (1886) and in dedicating parkland for his subdivisions, was lots of 25 x 100— "sometimes 30 feet," don't put sewers in unless required, "buy near an electric road, where you can get five-cent fares," and "Sell under market. Every man who buys a lot will be your salesman" (Davies 50, 70).

In short, although the mystery of the cultural chrysalis is ultimately impenetrable, we do know that the promulgation of the American front yard was not achieved institutionally from the top down. By the time the real estate business had its national (or even regional) voice, well before zoning ordinances had become accepted practice, and before Covenants, Conditions and Restrictions for subdivisions to regulate setbacks and fences became common, the vernacular front yard had become the norm. We know this, because of the attitude of the 1909 anonymous contributor to the *Atlantic*, who so clearly perceived herself as an unAmerican *agente provacatrice*, hoping to foment a revolution by the example of her English wall, giving backbone to the grumbling malcontent neighbors who she imagined to be secretly opposed to the tyranny of the lawn.

She was quite wrong. An unpredicted conflation of social, economic, technological and aesthetic developments and innovations had resonated with the American Dream. What American Dreamers saw as they trolleyed through proudly open subdivided vistas struck sympathetic vibrations like the profoundest of all myths, whose office is to reconcile opposites; in this case, to reconcile the paradox of the equally cherished values of nuclear family independence and of community cooperation, of private possession and of public pride.

57. Scottwood's handsome streets were featured in sumptuous albums and portfolios, as well as picture post cards. Collingwood Avenue was the real showplace. It is worth noting that unlike "house-portraits," street views are promotional statements by real estate companies and civic boosters. (Lake County Illinois Museum/Curt Teich Postcard Archives)

116 Front Yard America

58. A Scottwood-style upper middle-class development in St. Paul, Minnesota, all ready for sales. The houses were erected by Smith and Taylor in 1901; this photograph was published in 1902. (C.P. Gibson photo, Minnesota Historical Society)

59. When neighborhoods have alleys, as here in Minneapolis, the park-like lawnscape is uninterrupted by driveways and cars.

As Toledo Goes 117

60. How long does it take to grow shade trees? These 30-year shade trees on Blaisdell Avenue in Minneapolis were planted in 1890. (C.J. Hibbard photo, Minnesota Historical Society)

61. The streetcar on the left provided the impetus for the houses on the right. The street is a springtime morass, but sidewalks provide a neat border for the connected lawns, circa 1910. (Minnesota Historical Society)

118 Front Yard America

62. In 1890 Pictorial of *Waterloo Iowa* establishes the fact that contiguous yards were a midwestern high style at least some years earlier. This is the Residence of M. Frank Neely and View of South Street. (The Grout Museum of History and Science)

63. In Oak Park, Illinois, Frank Lloyd Wright's studio and home is designed for privacy...

64. ...but the houses he designed for neighbors have deep setbacks and spacious open lawns.

65. Possibly clients who were influenced by Wright's famous *Ladies' Home Journal* designs did not read the small print: street shrubbery was omitted from the *drawings* to provide a clear view of the house. Wright was wrong because that's what Americans wanted in three dimensions!

Part Eight

Myths and Anxieties

While it is true that myths can reconcile cultural and psychological contradictions and paradoxes in the best traditions of Claude Levi-Straus, Carl Jung and Joseph Campbell, this doesn't mean that the myths and their attendant rituals produce unmitigated contentment. One kind of tension was recognized at the very beginning by Frank Jesup Scott. Walls do not necessarily make good neighbors, but dispensing with them invites new violations, especially from boisterous children, and Bruno and Rover as well, as the *Atlantic* correspondent found out. To her, the myth of private property was a sham: "we have pretended long enough that we own a bit of out-doors." But five years later, Robert Frost in "Mending Wall" exposed the fallacy of the myth-sustaining ritual of spring wall mending and of the neighborliness of hard boundaries:

> '*Why* do they make good neighbors? Isn't it
> Where there are cows? But here there are no cows.
> Before I built a wall I'd ask to know
> What I was walling in or walling out,
> And to whom I was like to give offense.'
> Something there is that doesn't love a wall.

By mid-century, as we have seen, Elizabeth Gordon maintained that Americans' lives had changed to the degree that the fenceless myth was outworn. Formerly, she said, "Each identified himself with the whole.... These friendly extroverted gardens had their part in forming the friendly extroverted people...." but now Americans lived closer together and craved greater privacy. Her campaign to turn front yards into private living rooms failed, and it may well be that her error was in not recognizing that during the same years that the open front yard gained ascendancy the porch was assuming the function of the mediating space between the public front and the private living room. With the advent of the automobile, which brought noise and strangers whizzing by where strolling neighbors had passed before, the Back Yard Living Room and its subsequent avatars of Terraces, Patios and Decks provided privacy without sacrificing the communal statement in front.

As the twentieth century drew to a close, however, the tone of the arguments against the front yard changed. Trespassing, private ownership and personal privacy were not the salient issues of the last decade of the century, although they certainly are more than dormant concerns. It is the lawn itself and lawn mowing that are at the crux. Sara Lowen entitled a 1991 article in *American Heritage* "The Tyranny of the Lawn," and Michael Pollan in his sensitively entertaining *Second Nature, A Gardener's Education* in the same year asked the rebellious question *Why Mow?*" Both of these writings take in new complexities of environmental issues, but let us first examine the idea of *tyranny*. American lawns are tyrannical in two ways, social tyranny and maintenance tyranny. As Michael Pollan says, "Since we have traditionally eschewed fences and hedges in America, the suburban vista can be marred by the negligence—or dissent—of a single property owner. This is why lawn care is regarded as such an important civic responsibility in the suburbs, and why, as I learned as a child, the majority will not tolerate the laggard or dissident" (55ff). Pollan's father was more a dissident than a mere laggard, for one summer he stopped mowing altogether. Pollan remembers:

...I felt the hot breath of a tyrannical majority for the first time. Nobody would say anything, but you heard it anyway: *Mow your lawn*. Cars would slow down as they drove by our house. Probably some of the drivers were merely curious: they saw the unmowed lawn and wondered if perhaps someone had left in a hurry, or died. But others drove by in a manner that was unmistakably expressive, slowing down as they drew near and then hitting the gas angrily as they passed—this was pithy driving, the sort of move that is second nature to a Klansman. (20)

Pollan captures the insidiousness of neighborly psychological sanctions, something that I recall vividly and with upwellings

Myths and Anxieties 125

66. "Something there is that doesn't love a wall." Two visual examples of the oxymoronic "friendly fence." In one, the chainlink security fence secures nothing...

67. ...in the other, a neat picket stops where it could impede a clear view of the house and foundation.

126 Front Yard America

68. A whimsical *faux* gateway at Castle Howard in Yorkshire. It is on the edge of a four-foot ha-ha dropoff. The "gate," however, draws visitors along a graveled walk through the park and it frames the vista of the farmland.

69. A gate as pure ornament on a farm near Peoria. The aluminum filigree gate is supported by massive brick posts to the left of the driveway, but it is not related to the drive or walks. Far from separating private from public, its function seems only to punctuate the open lawn and coordinate with the filigree upper deck.

of remembered anxiety from my youthful days in Manitowoc, Wisconsin, where we lived in an attractive World War I housing development with elm-shaded curving streets and neat, two-story houses of some half-dozen variants on Dutch colonial, all painted white or moss-green (until 1947, when my mother decided we should paint ours barn-red with white trim; now *that* stopped the traffic!). My parents loved flowers and trees, but were only passable gardeners, and we were not a lawn-proud family. More laggards than dissidents were we.

The tyranny of the neighboring lawn aesthetic is intensified by an extremely critical time frame, for, to produce the Frank Scott effect (which *is* beautiful), when one homeowner mows his lawn, everyone on the block must follow within 24 hours. It is particularly important for those who have weedy lawns to conform, because brightly shining dandelions will interrupt the community carpet in a most jarring way, and further neglect will turn them to puffs spreading pollution indiscriminately. We lagged, and the unvoiced disapproval was palpable. Finally my brother or I would get out the always dull push-mower, and the anxiety would heighten. For one thing, because we were late, *our* lawn would now put the others to shame by being smoothly clipped. Another thing was the dilemma of the fenceless border. Should we mow an inch or few over Herzog's "line"? If you tried to hew to the line (which was invisible), there'd be a ragged edge; if you went over, was this an implication of encroachment? And most of all, was Mrs. Herzog watching with disapproval from behind the curtain? Matters were not much better in the back yard, where there was a three-foot high wire fence on the property-line. Herzog's had neatly clipped lawn up to the wire, we had a border garden (desultarily weeded), and at the back, a lilac hedge (invasively intolerant of legal boundaries).

Readers can probably supply their own examples of the social-psychological tyranny of the communal lawn, either from the viewpoint of the majority who are plagued with neighboring eyesores, or of those who march to different drummers, contributing the eyesores by neglect or alternative aesthetics. The tensions may be expressed overtly: consider the *Atlantic* contributor who built the high brick wall, or Ottalie Williams' recollection of neighbors who had to build high board fences to mask the "queer old ladies' " jungle, or Michael Pollan's story of owners of a half-million-dollar Maryland home who received an anonymous note *please, cut your lawn.* It is a disgrace to the entire neighborhood" (55), or the advice of Patricia Armstrong to others who want to replace a lawn with a native prairie to *Inform neighbors and city council before you start.* Send out a letter explaining all the good reasons why you are planting a prairie," and "When applying for a variance, avoid the word 'wild' " (63).

Thus, sustaining a myth that reconciles polar contradictions in a culture is replete with anxieties. You can't be individually independent and democratically equal without tension. It is a curious fact that American law contributes more to the tension than to its resolution. Whereas in England there are such traditions as "the old doctrine of common law known as the doctrine of ancient lights" whereby "a window that has had light coming into it for a certain amount of time is entitled to continue the enjoyment of that light" (Davis 108), in America "there is no right to light, air or view, unless it has been granted in writing by law (usually local) or subdivision rule.... This legal right that a property owner has no right to light, air or view has been favored in our country because it encourages building or expansion" (Jordan, Sections 8/3, 11). Cora Jordan's *Neighbor Law: Fences, Trees, Boundaries & Noise* provides information on the many ramifications of this *laissez faire* American tradition, but in general, neighbors have to work it out themselves, and tut-tuts, *moues*, pithy driving, and the other small-arms of community psychological warfare are probably more effective than taking legal recourse.

Turning from social tyranny to the tyranny of lawn maintenance, we should recognize that there are fanatics about lawns as there are among gardeners of roses, hostas and Hubbard squashes. Maintaining a weed-free, crisply-bordered, uniformly smooth greensward can be obsessive and addictive. Yard-addictiveness is not only American. Some years ago we found ourselves without room or bed on a Bank Holiday in Wales, but a kindly B & B host referred us to friends who put us up for the night. The man of the house was the equivalent of an American county agricultural agent, so I was curious about why he had paved his front and back yards with concrete. He explained that it was the only way he could go cold turkey, for his gardening addiction had been such that he was laboring by electric torch-light into the silent watches of the night to maintain weed-free beds for giant vegetable-marrows and prize-winning Miniver roses. Similar radical solutions are fairly common especially in the American desert areas of Arizona and California where lawn maintenance is an expensive battle against God's arid will. But for most Americans on that 30,000-plus square-mile lawnbelt from Maine to Mendocino, maintenance is not a maniacal obsession, but ranges from irritability when a spell of rain makes mowing a heavy chore, or a summer vacation brings one back to a primitive savannah, to Richard Wolkomir's macho satisfaction in performing one of the "last gender-affirming chores," to Scott's pastoral pleasure "pushing these grass-cutters over a velvety lawn, breathing the fresh sweetness of the morning air and the perfume of new mown hay...." I must confess to experiencing the full range to some degree every summer, for although my "home-grounds" are not in the vernacular yard style that is my main subject, I delight in leveling some two acres of native grasses, flowers, ferns, shrubs and trees into the semblance of a hillocky parkland enclosed within an eight-acre wildwood of birch, fir, spruce, poplar, aspen, pine, maple, honeysuckle, hazelnut, alder, pin-cherry, mountain ash, raspberries, thimbleberries, yellow violets, wood anemones, bluebells, cowslips, ferns and native and escaped grasses.

To a considerable extent, my sward of leveled weeds and grasses is closer to our aesthetic ancestor, Blenheim, than are the living astroturfs of the American suburbs. Anyone who has taken extended strolls at Blenheim, or Chatsworth or Castle Howard will be struck with fact that although the vistas suggest a flowing of smooth turf through spinneys, copses, glens and bosky hangers, the reality is more tree-free meadows and roughly mown weeds and grasses. The difference, of course, is scale. On your 25 x 30 front lawn, a dandelion, plantain, mullein or patch of quack grass stands out like a pimple on a cover-girl (as they would in the *formal* gardens that are incorporated into most English parklands), but within the Picturesque style's sweep of acres, punctuated with "eye-catcher" statuary and follies, the weeds become part of the subtleties of palette.

A brief summary is in order here. Although there has been some voiced criticism of the vernacular contiguous front yard from quite early, this has been spotty and only rarely by critics from within the landscape/garden establishment (e.g. designer Herbert Caparn in 1937; *House Beautiful* editor Elizabeth Gordon in 1951 and 1960).[32] Until recently these criticisms have primarily referred to property rights and rights to privacy, although Gordon certainly is also addressing aesthetic dull conformity as well, and in doing so, very likely represents the unpublished opinions of most professional landscape architects after Scott, the originator and lone champion. More recent criticism, cresting in the early 1990s, though, bases its criticisms on the tyranny of the lawn, the pressure to conform to a neighborhood style and the personal inconvenience in maintaining that style. Current additional arguments are based on technological developments since the 1950s. The first is that gasoline powered mowers have almost entirely supplanted the hand mower. No more whirring blades; rather, deafening noise pollution, air pollution and added burdens on the oil reserves. Even more serious is the fallout from Viet Nam; the use of selective chemical herbicides to ensure a weed-free carpet of grass. Related, of course, is the increased use of chemical fertilizers to keep that carpet thick and green. All that percolates into the ground, and presumably, the groundwater, abetted by the use of another precious and dwindling resource, pure drinking water, which is increasingly being dispensed onto lawns automatically by programmed sprinkler systems. So the weed-free, fertilized lush grass grows, to be cut evenly by the motorized mower. And the lawn clippings? Until the 1980s, out with the garbage into the overflowing landfills.

In short, the lawn has become more than a source of personal irritability and occasional neighborhood tiffs; it has become an enemy of the environment and a threat to posterity. On a yard-to-yard basis, each householder could ignore the threat, or, if you were an ecological true believer, you could take individual action. But in countless communities the crisis hit when ordinances forbade placing of garden and lawn debris out for trash collection. In arid communities, water restrictions virtually ended lawns.

A host of questions emerge. Can anything be done? Is this the end of an era? Can we go back? What has happened to myth and ritual of the American front yard? To the American Dream?

As to the first, the means of rectifying the ecological crisis are well known, simple and inexpensive. The catch, though, is that they require some changes of habits. Let's start with mowers. Electric mowers are cheaper, quiet and don't pollute the neighborhood atmosphere—that's done at the power plant! Hand mowers are making a modest comeback advertised with some of Frank Jesup Scott's pastoral verbiage, plus aerobics and calorie-counting. They are expensive compared to what they used to cost, and no one likes to pay more for something that makes *you* do the work. But with the higher quality alloys, they are lighter, sharper, and more efficient than their grandparents (although essentially the design is identical to the 1869 mowers). The price is about half that of an electric mower or a cheap gasoline model. If a market proves to be there, hand mowers are likely to see the kinds of improvements that bicycles have had with Shimano gears, for instance. For someone like me, who has a couple acres of rough terrain to mow, a handmower had better come equipped with a husky teenage girl or boy, but the vernacular yards are so small that power mowers never made much practical sense anyway. The catch is only that one must mow often, or it is very heavy going through the meadow.

How about herbicides? The American front lawn flourished for at least 75 years without them, so why not Just Say No? It would mean getting on your knees to dig dandelions and plantains—a job that's both tough and frustrating if they've really taken hold (I have places where if I'd use a broad-leaf killer, there'd be nothing left but bare ground; and who likes bare ground? Dandelions!). But there's a more powerful reason that herbicides and chemical fertilizers will be as hard to root out as the thistles and horsetail ferns that plague me. Michael Pollan learned this when he published an earlier version of "Why Mow?" in the *New York Times Magazine*: the lawn chemical industry is a multi-billion-dollar business, and they are mighty touchy about "irresponsible" criticisms of their service to a great American myth. Not unlike the National Rifle Association.

As to fertilizers, any environmentalist will tell you that recycling lawn clippings will kill two birds with one stone. Frequent mowing will put the clippings right where they should be; less frequent mowing means raking (or bagging) and composting, and eventually, rich recycling. Thus, there are simple, ecologically sound and inexpensive ways to sustain this national symbol of democratic community, and as with hand mowers, there is also the strong likelihood that the lawn industry, under pressure, will continue to work on products and processes that keep them in business and protect the environment. So we *can* keep the front yard.[33]

But do Americans really *want* to keep the front yard? Or have there been enough social, economic and demographic changes that the proud symbol of community is nothing but a wasteful, useless, energy-draining residue of lost values and forgotten meanings? It would hardly be without precedent; the British have an ironic euphemism for the houses of worship that nobody uses in the "Redundant Churches" Act. Are our front yards redundant? Are they like the almost empty rituals of the Fourth of July and Memorial Day, which have been readjusted to make three-day weekends; or Presidents' Day, that obscures the myths of national heroes into a generic excuse for post-Christmas shopping mall "events"? There is much to point in that direction.

One factor is simply the high cost of housing. The American Dream of the detached, single family home on its own plot of ground in a suburban community is more and more out of grasp for our growing population, and, in some regions, rendered impossible by a dwindling supply of available land. For the well-off middle class, larger semi-rural plots are being designed by landscape architects and serviced by Wonderlawn, *et alia*. Or they are gentrifying central city row houses that never had yards. The middle middle-class must settle for multi-dwelling condos, cunningly arranged all kitty-wampus to disguise their dismal architectural sameness among professionally maintained berms with trouble-free evergreens. Their real *front* yards are blacktopped parking areas with numbered spaces. For the lower middle classes, "working-men's" suburbs like Toledo's Brown's Addition are settled by upwardly mobile former inner-city dwellers with no tradition of yard maintenance and a habit for personal security that finds its expression in chain link fences—see-throughable, totally ineffective as deterrents to thieves and vandals, patently pricey, and chillingly metallic.

The cornerstone of the American Dream home, the family, has deteriorated alarmingly. The 1992 *World Almanac* reported that in 1960, only 4.2 percent of children lived with a *never-married* parent; 30 years later in 1990, the figure was 30.6 percent of all American children lived with never-married parents. Children living with one divorced parent increased from 23 percent in 1960 to a 1980 high of 85.2 percent and in 1990, 83.6 percent (944). What this undoubtedly means for yards is a sharply increased number of people without the money, time, equipment, experience and, most of all, *inclination* to care for a yard. Most are in apartments, many are in trailer parks. What dreams the children might have is hard to say, but they are provided with no dream models of suburban homes, such as primary school readers provided for American children until Dick and Jane were liquidated by pioneer political correctors in the early 1960s (Schroeder, *Outlaw Aesthetics*, "The Genesis of Dick and Jane," but especially 69, 85-93). Moreover, people have ceased to know how to *use* front yards. This may seem strange, since we have defined the front yard as primarily symbolic and ornamental, but I can explain the usefulness of front yards from my own nostalgic memories, for the lawn-mowing anxieties that I reported are only part of the picture.

Grownups used front yards as they used their front porches, to converse with neighbors as they sat in the shade or the cool of an evening, or as they mowed or watered the lawn or edged the sod along the walks. Ray Bradbury evokes the front porch and yard rituals exquisitely in *Dandelion Wine*. But I remember playing what we called "Knife" on the front lawn—*mumblety-peg* is the more usual term—with our local variant of "Baseball" wherein you'd flip your jackknife for singles, doubles, triples and home runs. Boys played marbles on the walk, girls, jacks and hopscotch, and up through teen years a home-grown variant on Ping-Pong and handball played with a tennis ball. Croquet and badminton were better in the backyard where our lawn didn't slant, but on dull summer days girls and boys alike would sit on our front lawn playing round card games like Authors, rummy, fan-tan. And for real idle hours, you could make clover blossom chains and look for four-leaf clovers. Twilight was for neighborhood activities on the street and through all the yards (except the "mean" neighbors who didn't want kids trundling about); "hidengoseek," "statues," "I'll draw the frying pan and who will poke?" "redlight, greenlight I hope to see a ghost tonight," and while light held, "pom-pom pullaway." All this I remember from Manitowoc before and after World War II, and much the same from the war years in Panama City, Florida, where we also sang old-time songs and gospel hymns, and where my father and mother, shockingly gone native, would sit in the front yard on Sunday mornings, reading papers, talking and drinking beer.

What has happened to such idyllic uses of front yards? Once again, the causes of their virtual disappearances are several, combining social and technological influences. Among social changes, the fracturing of the nuclear family is one influence, and the related increase in the number of families where both parents are fully employed must further render front yards into unused space. The informal activities of my nostalgia were possible because mom was always at home, and, except for school, so were we. By contrast today's day-care centers fill up what would have been front-yard free time for young children. With two working parents, even summer school vacations are not easy to convert to family time, and, given the likelihood that one or another parent works in the service sector (where one labors so others can relax, eat or play), the *Saturday Evening Post* cover pictures of the "family that plays together stays together" are pure fantasy. There is no common time to be together, whether in front yard, back yard or family room.

But my nostalgic picture of the well-used front yard seems even more fantastic today because of the image of security that it projects. Where were the pushers, flashers, abductors, muggers, rapists, looters and gun-wielding hopheads that now make inner city neighborhoods physically threatening, that increasingly precipitate Neighborhood Watch organizations in middle-class subdivisions and suburbs, and that are even causing uneasiness in small towns?

Today, the front yard seems to be a place of dangerous vulnerability rather than for idyllic cloud-gathering. This sinister image may be more a popular perception than a certain reality in many towns and neighborhoods (it's hard to imagine nefarious lurkings in the middle of a block-long front lawn, but even where there is not a clear and present danger, there has been a major change that substantially reduced the social security of front yards: the Mrs. Herzog's are no longer home keeping an eye on neighborhood activities).

Which introduces two technological factors that I believe have been the most effective forces in reducing the front yard to a burdensome ornament. These are air-conditioning and television. Of television I need say little to add to the rafts of statistics showing how many hours children, teenagers, and older adults spend watching. Every hour in front of the tube is an hour when they might have been outside. Air-conditioning has killed the rich front porch-culture of the American South, only continuing in the poorest of black neighborhoods. Front yard culture is gone as well. It is now some fifteen years since I first made an automobile trip from Northern Minnesota to central Tennessee, deliberately avoiding interstate highways because I was doing an impressionistic study of small town life. It was late June, and lovely summer weather all the way. As far as the southern border of Minnesota, I saw all kinds of front yard activities—families and neighborhood kids playing croquet, volleyball and badminton, people working on lawns or flowerbeds, little folks selling Kool-Aid from card-table "stores" on front sidewalks or dancing through the sprinkler showers, boys zooming around on their bicycles. These vignettes of people *using summertime* and using yards decreased rapidly as I went further south, until, in Nashville, it was as if some dread plague had descended upon domestic areas and wiped out the population.

They were all inside, cooled to the Comfort Zone.

I made a similar trip in 1990, through rural areas and towns from Minnesota through Iowa, central Illinois and Indiana and back through Wisconsin. The effect of air conditioning was almost universal, the only front yard activity being lawn-mowing. It is no wonder that we now hear of the Tyranny of the Lawn. It is no wonder that those who can afford it are turning over their lawns to commercial contractors. Front yards have become like Victorian parlors and formal dining rooms, expensive, unused, ornamental spaces that need to be kept tidy for the sake of appearances only. They are redundant, irritating, ecologically suspect, and possibly dangerous to personal security. Q., one might say, E.D. But it's not that simple.

Part Nine

Front Yard Futures:
Plus ça change, plus c'est la même chose

Without a doubt Americans were in the last decade of the twentieth century in a transition period regarding both front yard design and their attitudes towards front yards and external domestic space. But change is not likely to be sudden or startling. There are two reasons. One is that the fenceless close-clipped front lawn is simple and inexpensive to establish and maintain in most of the United States from the Atlantic coast to the western edge of the Great Plains and in much of the Rocky Mountains and the Northwest north of San Francisco Bay. Lawns need regular care, but rarely expert care such as gardens require. In arid and semi-arid areas, water is the primary (and increasingly prohibitive) cost; along the Gulf Coastal Plain, the "ideal" bluegrass cultivars need replacement with "bent" grasses. Maintaining a smooth sward on 25- to 50-foot lots is usually a matter of regular mowing and some watering. (However maintaining a *weed-free emerald carpet* is more costly and demanding.) The most drastic alternative, concrete paving, is expensive, ecologically suspect because of runoff, and, if it is to be aesthetically more pleasing than a parking lot, needs additional architectural improvements (e.g., walls, canopies, different levels, etc.). Bricks or flagstones will leave the weed problem at joints, and, where frost-heaving occurs, require back-breaking maintenance. Flowers and many shrubs are much more demanding than grass. Without knowledgeable care, a neighborhood eyesore will be as certain a result of a floral front as an unmowed lawn would be. Paradoxically, a lovely, abundant flower garden is unlikely to enhance real estate values and will surely scare off many prospective buyers. Flower gardens simply are too demanding for working families as Scott recognized over a century ago. Any combination of lawn with alternatives such as flower beds, flagged walks, concrete planters, walls or pools, still leaves the lawn "problem." (For some ten years we had a rowhouse in town with a 6 x 12-foot front lawn; all the tyrannies were there—

weeds, edging, watering in drought, and mowing in harmony with the neighbors—only with less space to maneuver a mower.)

I'll return to alternative front yard designs, but first we should look into the other reason that there is unlikely to be a sudden change from the vernacular norm. America's domestic landscape of detached single-family dwellings in towns, city neighborhoods, subdivisions and suburbs is the result of a century-long building expansion. From circa 1875 to circa 1975 all the moderately priced houses were sited according to a plan that *assumed* fenceless, contiguous front lawns. Lots were of limited width and houses were set back from the street and sidewalk. *Ergo*, that underlying design is what there is to work with now, unless we move the houses, re-draw property lines and re-route streets. And while potentially anarchy might be allowed to reign within a block of six or eight houses each with a unique front design, propinquity absolutely forces the acknowledgment of at least some community conventions. Consider neighbors A, B, C, D, E and F. "A" wants to surround his yard with a three-foot brick wall; "B" wants a six-foot cast-iron fence; "C" raises Pekinese and wants a chain-link fence; "D" wants a natural prairie-yard of native species; "E" wants a floral border; and "F" wants a neatly clipped privet hedge enclosing a lawn with weeping birches centered on either side of the sidewalk. Every place where there is a shared border, there must be some agreement. The conjunction of the brick wall and adjacent cast-iron fence will produce neither owners' desired effects; the "prairie" and herbaceous border will be in continuous conflict. By contrast, the normal vernacular tradition establishes a general consensus, with quite broad options within one's own front yard. Indeed, one reason that it takes a practiced eye to see the underlying vernacular pattern in older neighborhoods is that there is such variety among the choice and placement of specimen trees, flower beds, foundation plantings, low hedges, mock fencelets, chain-link fences and the decorative jetsam of concrete urns, plastic flamingoes, bird baths and fiberglass deer. In short, there is almost anarchical latitude for self-expression that evolves with the neighborhood. It is new neighborhoods where the tyranny is most pronounced, largely because the fresh sodding begs for loving care and both individual and neighborhood pride.

Thus, the American vernacular style is likely to persist because it is relatively cheap and relatively easy to maintain, and because the real estate of America has been laid out to accommodate that style. It is indeed such a very close matching of layout and style that the adaptation of alternative designs from professional landscapers is rarely effective. By the time the average homeowner has scaled down the corporate and private estate professional landscape designs to fit into a 25- to 50-foot wide lot, with a one- or two-story vernacular house (Queen Anne, bungalow, Dutch Colonial, four-square, Levittown cottage, ranch, rambler, etc.), with the house still firmly set back 15-40 feet from the street that it faces, and with the obligatory driveway and garage for practically any post-1925 housing development (by the 1960s, often dwarfing the house itself)—by the time the homeowner has made the adjustments and compromises dictated by those givens—the alternative design is ludicrous, if we can recognize what it seeks to imitate, or simply pathetic, if we can't. Further, in the manner of trickle-down popular culture, the vernacular versions tend to be in "last season's style." The *berm* is a case in point. (The term is an eighteenth-century coinage having to do with fortifications and later applied to canal towpaths.) Resurrected in the 1960s and 1970s as an alternative to an exposed front yard or as a kind of sound barrier, reduced to a cliché in the 1980s to relieve the monotony of suburban apartment-house complexes, by 1992, *Landscape Architecture* entitled one of their articles on midwest landscape architecture "Berm: A Four-Letter Word." Debra L. Mitchell, president-elect of the American Society of Landscape Architects talked with some Midwestern architects about whether there is a Midwestern landscape heritage. [The answer is yes: Jens Jensen out of Olmsted out of Downing out of Repton.] Unfortunately, instead of using the heritage, architects have "the standard look."

"Describe the 'standard look'," said Mitchell.
"A suburban landscape," said Ryan, "as opposed to urban. It's Kentucky bluegrass—"
"Wall to Wall," interjected Mitchell.
"—with berms, and probably no sense of enclosure to the site. Large deciduous trees, 'large' meaning large caliper when installed. Not a lot of ground cover plants. 'Seasonal' accents at the entry. And occasional boulder fountains. It's the corporate look." (Leccese 69)

What berms become in the vernacular is what Karen Koegler, looking at yards in Lexington, Kentucky, characterized as "disassociated heaps of mulch" (11). In Duluth, Minnesota, the first small-property berm was installed in the early 1980s by an architect in front of his Queen Anne house facing prestigious London Road—which is also U.S. 61. The purpose is clearly visual and auditory privacy, which it probably achieves, although the image to some passersby may be that of an impersonal heap of mulch. But that's as it should be, if your goal is privacy rather than publicity. More recent imitations, however, miss the functional goal, because they are too low to be barriers to vision or sound. What they do is to accent nicely the neat lawn between the berm and the foundation planting! In short, we are right back at the front yard as neighborhood ornament. An even more emphatic instance of the difficulty of changing the deeply-rooted inherent character of the American front yard is across London Road from the architect's house. (This was an 1890 streetcar suburb called Lester Park; houses on the southside have dramatic frontage on Lake Superior and many are on spacious lots, but the majority of the homes were fairly modest middleclass frame structures on small lots.) The front yard in question dispensed entirely with a lawn, replacing it with landscape-timber terraces. The owner goes

Overall, these bear the marks of the plans of professional landscape architects, and yet she concludes that "while there is an attempt at closure, the space has still not become one for private enjoyment: this is not a courtyard movement" (6-7, 11).

Although my purpose throughout has been to describe, not prescribe, I cannot resist speculating on ways of making the narrow front yard into some sort of outdoor living room without recourse to high unfriendly walls. Privacy screens are becoming more and more common in backyards, and so, clearly, one could do something similar in front. A California landscape architect was able to achieve a front enclosed courtyard on his 50 x 100-foot lot without violating the city's 20-foot setback requirement. "I've managed to build a patio *and* make a welcoming landscape," Chris D. Moore wrote in *Fine Gardening*. "I walled in the patio without making a fortress that would shun the neighborhood" (30). Wayne Renaud and his design-firm partner achieved something of the same type on their 25-foot lot in Toronto, described as their "Welcoming Waters" entry. Also in 1992, *Southern Living* magazine offered a "garden bonus" section entitled "Fix Up the Front Yard." The main thrust here is not to attack the vernacular lawn (although "The smaller you make your lawn, the less work you'll have maintaining it"), but to get homeowners to ask first what they want lawns, shrubs, entry paths, doorways, walls, etc. to *do* for them, and then to ask which shrubs, what layout, what materials are needed. This is not the normal process of a national vernacular style where the arrangement is a traditional given. It is, though, the process of good architects, and all *Southern Living*s case studies were done by members of ASLA. Some appear to be rather large projects, but of a smaller one in Alabama, the article concludes (italics mine):

Planted in the spring of 1990, the yard is *the toast of the neighborhood*. "The *neighbors across the street* are thrilled," states James, "because they've been living there for 45 years and this is the first time *this yard* has *looked right*." (74)

beyond a green thumb; it is positively iridescent. Bulbs, rhizomes, perennials, annuals, flowering shrubs and trees almost hide the house. The effect, however, is not at all one of privacy, but of public display of an iridescent thumb. This front garden also provides an instance of the phenomenon of vernacular diffusion of innovation. Within about two blocks there are three yards that were influenced by this almost Henri Rousseau-like jungle of floriculture. One is fairly successful, though the thumb is only a dull green. Another just has shrubs planted heavily on the sides of the front walk. The third is seeking a maintenance-free front yard with wide-spreading low evergreens slowly covering the mulch. And that's it. The residential part of London Road is some 40 blocks long, and except for heavily wooded yards and some professionally landscaped estates on the Lake side, the berms and floral terraces have barely dented the American way of yards, at least on smaller lots.

Karen Koegler's examination of an "upscale neighborhood" of smallish houses of the 1930s and 1940s in Lexington in 1991 showed a pattern of elements that are producing a "softening of the front yard." The elements will bear comparison with Gordon and Howland's "American style" in *House Beautiful* 40 years earlier. Some elements:

> *asymmetry;
> *elaboration of the entry;
> *few straight lines marking edges;
> *removal of foundation plantings;
> *replacement with shrubs like hollies chosen for texture, color and growth characteristics;
> *curvilinear planting beds circumscribing more lawn area;
> *greater use of ground covers;
> *more flowers;
> *specimen trees like the redbud and dogwood which provide spring and fall color;
> *small groves of trees, often obscuring or sheltering the entry.

What is significant in these articles is the recognition of the function of *welcoming*, the acknowledgment of being part of a neighborhood, and the direct involvement of neighbors' opinions. Still, these are professional designers and they are not making do with "ready-to-wear" materials from the local discount lumber store or garden center. These articles, incidentally, rarely hint at what professional landscaping costs, but in a *Fine Gardening* "A Front-Yard Makeover; Good fences make good neighbors," designer Michael Glassman tips his hand:

Installing the landscape was relatively simple but time-consuming-full-time work for two months for my crew of three. To prepare the area, we removed the cherry tree, killed the lawn with herbicide and dug it out, jackhammered out the old driveway, and leveled the site. Then we built the fence.... (64)

and presumably made better neighbors for the client. It *is* a beautiful court yard, but just figure out the cost of almost 1,000 worker hours and heavy equipment subcontracting.

The Moore and Renaud articles also show two "unAmerican" characteristics—one is *in-turning vision* and the second is *miniaturization of vista*. There are both aspects of what Edward T. Hall named *proxemics*, the "Hidden Dimension," the psychological perceptions of space that are deeply imbedded in us by our cultures. Traditional Japanese landscaping, of course, is the example *par excellence* of in-turning vision and miniaturized vistas. And all courtyard cultures do the same thing in different ways—Persian, Moorish, Spanish, Provencal, Italian and other primarily Mediterranean societies have enclosed little landscapes within their houses, open to the sky, but not to strangers. It is more than a matter of climate that even where Americans have built houses up to the public roadway or walkway, the only places where courtyards were included are in French New Orleans and Mobile and in the Spanish Southwest where the Romance language vernaculars predominated. Fly over Manhattan and you'll see New York's courtyard in Central Park; hardly a place of in-turning vision and miniaturized vistas! In patterning American suburban design after an English aristocratic tradition, Olmsted and Vaux opted for expanded vistas, and when Scott democratized it into an aesthetic for working class subdivisions, he found a means of having it both ways with small land-parcels and long vistas. Another paradox. And yet another, for paradoxically we *can* reform the vernacular front yard, but yet we *can't*. We *can* because the examples are there, not only in recent *Fine Gardening* articles, but for at least a quarter-century in countless *Sunset* Californizations of the Japanese traditions and in many back yard schemes listed in *Readers' Guide* as "Outdoor Rooms, Decks, Patios and Terraces." Yet we *can't* reform, because it would require a revolution—literally a 180-degree turn—in vision and vista, for our houses—urban, suburban and rural alike—face the public thoroughfares, our picture windows frame the view of houses across the way, our foundation plantings are invisible to the indwellers, our yard and garden ornaments—even objects of veneration—are oriented to passersby,[34] and our laws deny private rights to light, air and view. All of which constitutes a truly formidable array of forces of inertia. And there are other powerful forces. A century of mass marketing in real estate. Ordinances and restrictive deeds to frustrate attempts to circumvent the norm. A multi-billion dollar yard and lawn industry invested in the tradition. And a lot of people who *like* to look at, to maintain, and to seek the ever-closer achievement of the Ideal, a carpet of *almost* natural astrotruf from sea to shining sea.

True, there are powerful counter-forces as well. The entire American Society of Landscape Architects. Ecologists. An economy that no longer nurtures single-family lower income dwellings. Family structure in disarray. Ordinances restricting water usage, chemical additives and organic waste disposal. And more and more lay critics of the Tyranny of the Lawn.

But Newton's Laws of Motion are not the only way to approach problems of inertia and counter-forces. More applicable from the realm of chemical law is Le Chatelier's Principle, for it looks at the inertia of *systems*, and as we have seen, the front yard in America is not a monolith, but a complex system of climate, natural resources, botany, aesthetic theories and practices, economics and industry, real estate marketing, local ordinances and human behaviors, traditions and values. Stated simply, Le Chatelier's Principle says that a system in equilibrium when disturbed by a factor will produce a reaction that will tend toward equilibrium. The greater amount of the introduced factor, of course, the more the equilibrium will tend in that direction. Applying this to the vast system that is a nation's landscape style, it will be seen it takes powerful innovations to disturb the equilibrium, but regardless of how it changes, *plus ça change, plus c'est la même chose*. This is what Karen Koegler observed in Lexington and what I see in my daily drives along London Road and Glenwood Street. Elizabeth Gordon's fulminations in mid-century disturbed a very self-satisfied system. While it has taken a long time to see changes, things are not the same now, however much of the American neighborhood vernacular landscape is still a recognizable national style. Koegler, for example, perceptively observes that foundation plantings are still there; they've just moved forward onto the berm!

What does the future hold? Pluralism, I think, is the answer. There will be perfect neighborhoods of contiguous lawns, just as one can still find in Fergus Falls, Minnesota, a city whose arching elms lovingly defended by civic ordinances make a gothic nave of residential streets. Regional differences will become more pronounced, especially in drier climates. I shall not be surprised to find communities that will enshrine fencing or dividing walls as Duany and Plater-Zyberk have already dictated to some of their post-modern communities (Dean, *passim*). The "softened" front yard will predominate partly because of the tremendous growth of the professional landscaping industry. As more and more modest-sized places are professionally re-done in Elizabeth Gordon's and the ASLA/

"American Style," there will be more and more vernacular limitations. But another reason for softening is that there are likely to be fewer lower income single-family developments and neighborhoods will be older. As young trees mature, the boundary lines that are so entrenched in plat books and tax rolls will become dappled, shaded and softened. Established neighborhoods, as I've said, require a trained eye to see the underlying pattern.

Who knows? Someone may look back at Frank Jesup Scott's Plate XXII and see that in truth, nobody actually followed his plan, which called for a border of informally placed clumps of shrubs and trees along the sidewalk, and *then* the ribbon of communal lawn. He never intended a public face for all our houses.

It just happened that way.

Why has America invented its *own* Style in Gardens?

by Dr. Joseph E. Howland
House Beautiful's Garden Editor

The automobile changed our living habits

Twenty-five years ago we abandoned our gardens to go for a "Sunday drive." Today we seek refuge from bumper-to-bumper traffic. So we convert our own back yards into comfortable areas for lounging, eating, and entertaining.

Houses are growing smaller

America craves the luxury of spaciousness, but rising costs force us to shrink the size of the house. So we use big windows and livable gardens to make small houses seem larger.

Power equipment replaces the professional gardener

The garden now is designed to eliminate the need for professional gardeners. This banishes all the fussy garden details that past generations loved. Lawns become big open sweeps, edged with mowing strips. Flowers are confined to show areas.

America's pace makes a place for relaxing essential

Americans spend so much time on the run that they must have an adequate place for relaxing. Now the garden is being redesigned to serve as a quiet room for relaxing.

Americans are sun-lovers and fresh-air enthusiasts

Everyone in America strives to live outdoors as much as possible. Most people, especially children, must do this right in their own back yards, so the garden takes on a new importance. It becomes a recreation spot useful to the whole family.

Here's what our style produced ⟶

70. Elizabeth Gordon and Joseph Howland's extensive feature in the February 1951 *House Beautiful* heralded a New Look in yards and gardens: The American-Style! This brief analysis of causes combines the effects of technology, economics and behavior quite accurately. It is illuminating to compare the analyses with F.J. Scott's from 80 years earlier.

150 Front Yard America

—or the whole Neighborhood?

71. "Who owns your front yard? You—or the whole neighborhood?" (Courtesy *House Beautiful*). With this challenge in 1960 editor Elizabeth Gordon of *House Beautiful* launched an aggressive campaign for front yard privacy by way of hedges, fences and berms.

72. Why berm is a four-letter word. Too low for privacy from curious eyes, not extensive enough to eliminate grass mowing, and ineffective as a sound barrier because the two-car driveway opens everything anyway.

Front Yard Futures 151

73. A recent front yard alternative that is frustrated by the givens of a street car suburb: narrow lot fronting a street and neighbors marching to the dominant drummer. Note the left property line.

74. An ambivalent sign of the later twentieth century. The openness, honesty and friendliness of the democratic vernacular front yard are given the lie, and yet the Neighborhood Crime Watch programs seek to preserve traditional ideals by means of traditional neighborliness and volunteerism.

152   Front Yard America

75. The Levittown developments of the GI-Bill post-war years were roundly chastised for cheap, mass-produced conformity. Identical houses on identically featureless lawns have matured into individually remodeled homes and personalized yards. A practiced eye, though, will discern the underlying 1-1/2-story houses and the vernacular standard yards. Thus the American paradox of individual freedom and egalitarian democracy is sustained.

Front Yard Futures 153

76. This advertisement from the May 1990 *Horticulture* nicely sums up the American Style for the century's end. The lawns are weed-free carpet with few impediments to almost effortless mowing. The house on the left achieves Elizabeth Gordon's approach to privacy with shrubbery in front. The other two have open front yards but the middle has hedges and planters around the rear patio, while the third uses a high fence and trees. Front yards, though, are no longer living rooms. They are public ornaments. (Courtesy John Deere Corporation)

NOTES

[1] Ann Leighton speaks of two peculiarly American features of landscaping, "foundation planting" and "the suburban custom of uniting the front lawns of however many houses there may be on both sides of a street to present an untroubled aspect of expansive green to the passerby....": 249. See note 8 for indications of regional exceptions to the national norm.

[2] See Upton for a critical and analytical history of topics and methods in the study of vernacular buildings.

[3] Marie Luise Gothein's authoritative *A History of Garden Art* (1928) says "the modern American taste for a wide set-back did not develop until after the Civil War....As soon as pioneer conditions began to wane...the picket fences also disappeared. For although they were retained for a time on custom, there presently arose the counter style of having front yards all open to the street—a style which has ruled ever since" (439).

The paucity of evidence about vernacular landscapes is not only American. W.G. Hoskins, in his authoritative *The Making of the English Landscape* encountered the problem in trying to reconstruct pre-1790 heathland pastures (190-195).

[4] cf. Dwight: "The usual lawn expresses nothing so much as a vacancy of mind." John Stilgoe, on the other hand, maintains that "only the rare critic condemned typical borderland street edged with trees and lawns sweeping uninterrupted up to houses, and more important, sweeping along parallel to the street itself," *Borderland,* 198. While I agree these are rare, rarer still are *advocates* of this typical arrangement. In short, it was ignored by the professionals, except by the implied opposition of their never designing such a front yard.

A 1908 champion of the fenceless state was one Ada March, who wrote in *American Homes and Gardens* that "the fenceless garden never misses the fence, the well-kept border, the carefully cut grass being all that is needed."

[5]The introduction and shifts in nomenclature in *Readers Guide to Periodical Literature* on various extensions to the home are informative:
1904 "Porch-parlors"
1905 "Back Yards"
1907 "Outdoor Living Room" [porch]
1919 "Outdoor Living Room" [garden]
1933 "Back Yards—See Outdoor Living Room"
1939 "Terraces"
1957 "Decks—See Outdoor Living Room"
1976 "Decks, Patios, Terraces" replaces "Outdoor Rooms"
Not surprisingly, 1955-1957, the cresting of suburban tract developments also was the crest for articles on "Outdoor Rooms" (84), "Lawnmowers" (27), and "Barbecue" (47). In the entire span of publication, looking under the above subject-headings as well as "Lawns," "Home Grounds," and "Landscape Gardening," only three articles had titles referring to *front* yard (*House Beautiful*, April 1954) *front* lawn (*House Beautiful*, May 1960), *front* landscape (*Flower and Garden*) March 1980).

[6]"Like a carpet," said *Scientific American* in an 1875 article on "A Good Lawn."

[7]In an article on "Schoolhouse Reading" I found it useful to distinguish *folk* vernacular from *mass* vernacular architecture. "Folk vernacular is traditional and native down to the very materials used," while "Mass vernacular is identifiable primarily by the use of commercial machine-made materials." Applying this to vernacular landscape architecture it is possible (even likely) to have an instinctive yard design, i.e., a *traditional form*, executed by the home-owner and/or local contractors using "store-bought" shrubs, grass-seed, fertilizer, trellises, concrete blocks and rented tools and handbooks from the public library. The lines between vernacular and what Upton calls academic architecture become hazy in the upper middle income bracket. May Thielgaard Watts' "Stylish House—Revisited" is one of the finest depictions of the historic evolution of American yards from 1856 to 1985, but in none of the seven stages of development is the yard without a fence or hedge, although it always has an expansive lawn. Is the "stylish" house and yard vernacular? By 1906 the fictional residents of Watts' stylish house were doing their yard in accordance with the rules laid down by a garden club lecturer. In 1960, the more

recent fictional residents use a landscape architect for this rather large lot in Illinois.

⁸According to the 1990 *Statistical Abstracts*, (719) in 1987 60 percent of housing units (N=102,652,000) were Single Family Detached homes; 47 percent of all units were *Owner Occupied* Single Family Detached; only 12 percent of total housing was in structures of 10 and more units.

The regional breakdown of Single Family Detached (owner/renter occupied) is Northeast 50 percent; Midwest 68 percent; South 66 percent; West 60 percent. The median year for when the units were built was 1962; the Northeast is well below the median for other regions at 1950. Other notable differences between the Northeast and other regions are the percent of Single Family Attached [row houses] 7.3 percent vs. 4-5 percent; and structures of 50+ units; 8 percent vs. 2-3 percent.

⁹Caparn writes at length about the back yard. For the front, he deplores the popular penchant for foundation plantings (cf. Gothein, 440-41 and fig. 662). His plan for a representative yard indicates a hedge around the perimeter, which strangely doesn't identify by species. The yard has 25 different floral cultivars and 25 different trees and shrubs!

¹⁰A pointed example is in Oak Park, Illinois, where there is the largest concentration of Frank Lloyd Wright homes, including his own home and studio which has a shrub and tree-filled yard enclosed by a brick wall for privacy and nature. Having the architect's model as a neighbor had no effect; none of his clients' houses is walled in, and most have spacious open lawns. Cf. Sprague (21, 25, 26, 27). The Hills House (28) and (28) and Furbeck House (61) have knee-high retaining walls at the front walk, not at all enhancing privacy. However, Wright's highly influential "Prairie House" designs in turn of the century *Ladies Home Journal* have absolutely clear, broad front lawns. Closer scrutiny of the design for four houses built on one block shows that while open to the *street*, the lawns have heavily shrubbed dividers separating neighbors. Finally Wright explains that his drawings omit "foliage of curb parkways to better show the scheme."

¹¹The Zoning Movement which originated in Germany was in full swing in the period 1912-1917. See *American City* articles of Bettman, Gabelman, Geyer, Haldeman, "Set-Back Lines." The first comprehensive zoning law in the United States was in New York City

in 1916, Davis (58). The actual influence of deed restrictions early in the century was negligible, Davies (65-69). I discuss this in Chapter VII.

[12]"What gives the vernacular way of life its vitality and persistence is its ability to adjust to circumstances, to external factors beyond its control...." (21).

[13]An endeavor to change the ways of the English vernacular style of walled, hedged, floral front yards provides telling support for the deeply rooted national preferences. In the 1920s and 1930s British landscape architects advocated the development of American-style contiguous open lawns. "Every endeavor should be made at the outset of a scheme to persuade tenants that fences or hedges, separating them from one another and from the road, are not a necessity, and that when every front garden is open there is little tendency to trespass. This may necessitate the society [i.e., "building society" = U.S. savings and loan] or authority owning the houses taking over the care of front gardens.... It is enough to bring tears to the eyes of the designer of houses to see what should be a simple lawn mutilated by constellations of flower beds," James and Yerbury (9-10). English householders have thwarted such attempts everywhere with hedges, walls, fences, arbors and beddings, fore and aft. Cf. Maxwell (455) for another instance of English upper-class opposition to "the hedged-off houses of the English towns, with their garden walls topped with broken bottles to warn away the cats and other marauders."

[14]On grassless yard traditions, see Jeane. For native American "yards," Nabokov and Easton: 66, 211, 214, 335. Early pioneer, Taft: 291, 429.

[15]Possibly the most negative position on yards, both front and back, were the 1879 articles on "New York Yards," presumably written by an editor of *The American Architect and Building News*. He advocates the elimination of all yards because they are useless. The only real justification for back yards was for clothes-drying, something that now are "expensive arrangements." Costlier houses have artificially heated drying rooms, and "we may remember also that clothes can as well be dried on the top of the houses as in a yard, and indeed better, in so far as the air there is purer and moves more freely." The arguments are explicitly economic, referring to Manhattan land-costs: 163-164. We may assume that the development of indoor

toilets was another factor, though the author makes no mention of outhouses.

[16]Erving Goffman's discussion of "performance teams" in chapter two of *The Presentation of Self* is perfectly applicable to neighborhoods and their presentation of front yards as community expressions. See especially 79-83. See my "Democratic Yard and Garden," especially 114-115 for the neighborhood commitment to a proper front yard.

[17]The bibliography at the end of this essay includes a variety of photographs, maps, paintings, etc. that have appeared in *American Heritage* and other publications listed under the headings of: "American City," "Atlas," "Before Urban Renewal," "Boosting the West," Brownlow, Cable, "Celebration of Cities," Davidson, Gowans, "Horace Engle's Candid Camera," "House Hunting," Jacob, Kouwenhoven *passim*, Reps *passim*, "Small Bright World," Taft, Stilgoe *passim*.

[18]The emphasis is mine. Historic reconstructions of this sort of enclosed flower and herb garden include the Whipple House in Ipswich, MA (1683), Tullie Smith House in Atlanta GA (circa 1840) and Celia Thaxter's garden on Appledore Island, ME (1894). McGuire: 9-15, 80-85. C.F. Thaxter, *passim*.

[19]The 1956 MGM film *The Swan* shows the process.

[20]Tice states that Chadborn and Coldwell produced 15,000 mowers in 1874: 64-65.

[21]The accelerated acceptance of the lawnmower and its effect on the landscape is an excellent example of George Kubler's "fast time."

[22]J.B. Jackson's *American Space* briskly summarizes the influence of fence laws on yards of the 1860s. I think he anticipates by about a decade because of the need for cheap, effective mowers. Harper reports that the U.S. Commissioner of Agriculture in 1871 recommended fencing cattle rather than fields: 224.

[23]On the history of the Mall, see Longstreth.

[24]*Consumers' Research Bulletin*, Apr. 1949: 8, 22-23; Aug. 1950: 9-12; *Consumer Reports 1948 Buying Guide*, 254-259, 309, 406, 407; *Consumer Reports 1949 Buying Guide*, 306-310.

[25]Hartford, Connecticut's Bushnell Park preceded Central Park in 1853, Jackson, *American Space*, 216.

[26]Most of the information on Scott's life and that of his father is derived from clippings and manuscripts in the Local History Department of the Toledo-Lucas County Public Library. A newspaper

clipping (1883?) alludes to the Parisian lady as his "partner for life"; the *National Cyclopedia of American Biography* tells of a divorce "some years" after the marriage.

[27] The evidence, unfortunately, is negative, although of course the grid was the favored American urban plan from Penn's design for Philadelphia in 1683. Possibly Downing had seen plans for midwestern railroad towns. See Morris, chapter 9. Stilgoe's *Borderland* seems to show the emergence of the "working mens" suburbs in the 1870s, see chapter 13, "Chicago."

[28] The date is speculative but probably accurate. The 1875 *Illustrated Historical Atlas has* "before and after" bird's-eye of Brown's Addition in 1870 and 1874. The first is forest, ponds and swamp; the second, with the juncture of three railroads on the out skirts is cleared, drained and has some small houses.

[29] Brown's Addition "platted with meeting the wants of the large population with moderate means, specially including working classes. To this end, the lots in price were brought within reach of many who were then hopeless of homes of their own," Waggoner, Vol. 1, 421.

[30] See Cora Jordan's 1991 *Neighbor Law: Fences, Trees, Boundaries & Noise* for a legal update on the endless American conflict.

[31] For example, The Curt Teich Postcard archives of the Lake County Museum in Wauconda, Illinois has a half-dozen Scottwood street views from around 1905-1910.

[32] Gothein (1928) and Leighton (1987) acknowledge the national typicality of the deep set back and open-faced lawns, but without any negative criticism. See notes 1 and 3, above.

[33] Bormann, Balmori and Geballe's *The American Lawn: An Environmental Anachronism* is devoted to "environmentally friendly" lawns.

[34] My chapter on "The Democratic Yard and Garden" in *Outlaw Aesthetics* discusses the history and meanings of American popular yard ornaments. There have been many studies since then of flamingos, concrete geese, nautical ornaments, etc.

WORKS CITED

Alberti, Leon Battista. *On the Art of Building in Ten Books*. Trans. Joseph Rykwert, Neil Leach, Robert Tavernor. Cambridge: MIT, 1988.

Allen, Frederick L. "Our National Shabbiness." *House Beautiful* 37 (Jan. 1915): 33-36.

"The American City. A Gathering of Turn-of-the Century Paintings." *American Heritage* 27.3 (Apr. 1976): 26-49. Everett Shinn tenement yards, 29.

Architectural Digest. *Gardens*. Los Angeles: Knapp, 1983.

Armstrong, Patricia K. "Prairie by Design: An Illinois Landscape Recalls Its Origins." *Fine Gardening* 19 (May/June 1991): 62-65.

Artwork of Toledo, Ohio 1895. Chicago: Parish Publishing Co., 1895.

Atlas of Perry County, Indiana, 1861.

Atlas of Kosciusko County, Indiana, 1879.

Atlas of Vigo County, Indiana, 1874.

Atlas of Sangamon County, Illinois, 1874.

Baist s Survey of Toledo, 1904.

"Before Urban Renewal." *American Heritage* 24.4 (June 1973): 28-35. William Chappel paintings of New York, circa 1810.

Bergman, Edward F. *Woodlawn Remembers: Cemetery of American History*. Utica: North Country Books, 1988.

Bettman, Alfred. "Residential Districts and the Courts." *American City* Aug. 1914: 113-115.

Bond, James, and Kate Tiller. *Blenheim, Landscape for a Palace*. Wolfeboro, NH: Alan Sutton, 1989.

"Boosting the West." *American Heritage* 36.6 (Oct./Nov. 1985): 34-41. Joseph Stimson photos, 36-37, of Diamondville, Wyoming in 1903.

Borman, F. Herbert, Diana Balmori and Gordon Geballe. *The American Lawn: an Environmental Anachronism?* New Haven: Yale UP, 1992.

Brownlow, Kevin. "The Day Before Hollywood." *American Heritage* 35.1 (Dec. 1983): 24-31. Photo on 31 of 1916 bungalows.

Bumgarner, Gay McDonnell. "10 Front Landscapes to Study or Copy." *Flower and Garden* Mar. 1980: 30-35.

Cable, Mary. "Buildings for Sale: Unexpected Beauty from a City Archive." *American Heritage* 30.5 (Aug./Sept. 1979): 66-77. Views of New Orleans houses. 76-77 board fences.

Caparn, Harold A. "City Lawns." *The Independent* 4 May 1918: 212, 224.

———. "The Average Yard; The Story of a Fifty-Foot Lot." *Arts and Decoration* Mar. 1937: 42-43, 53.

"Care of Lawns." *Scientific American* 18 May 1872: 231.

"A Celebration of Cities." *American Heritage* 30.2 (Mar./Apr. 1979): 14-25. Bird's-eye view of Cripple Creek in 1896, 22-23.

City Atlas of Toledo, Ohio. Philadelphia: G.M. Hopkins, 1881.

City of Toledo, Ohio Through a Camera. Toledo: Franklin Printing & Engraving, 1907.

Clark, Emily. "Own Your Own Home: S.E. Gross, The Great Domestic Promoter." Abstracts of the 1992 Winterthur Conference [on] *The American Home: Material Culture, Domestic Space, Family Life*. Winterthur Museum, Delaware, Oct. 29, 30, 31, 1992.

Coldwell Lawn Mowers (catalog). Newburgh, NY, 1912. This catalog, containing a history, is at the New York Public Library.

"Coldwell, Thomas." *National Cyclopedia of American Biography* 8: 65. New York: James T. White, 1900.

Cottage Residences, Rural Architecture and Landscape Gardening. 1842. Library of Victorian Culture: Watkins Glen, 1967.

Crouch, David, and Colin Ward. *The Allotment*. London: Faber & Faber, 1991.

Curtis, James R. "The Most Famous Fence in the World; Fact and Fiction in Mark Twain's Hannibal." *Landscape* 28.3 (1985): 8-14.

Curtis, James, and David Helgren. "Yard Ornaments in the American Landscape: A Survey Along the Florida Keys." *Journal of Regional Cultures* 4.1 (Spring/Summer 1984): 78-92.

Dary, David. *Cowboy Culture; A Saga of Five Centuries*. New York: Knopf, 1981.

Davidson, Carla. "The View from Fourth and Olive." *American Heritage* 31.1 (Dec. 1979): 76-93. Photos by St. Louis photographer Thomas Easterly. 80-81 for board fences.

Davies, Pearl Janet. *Real Estate in American History*. Washington: Public Affairs P, 1958.
Davis, Howard. "Explicit Rules, Implicit Rules, and Formal Variation in Vernacular Building." *Perspectives in Vernacular Architecture*. 4th ed. Thomas Carter & Bernard L. Herman, U of Missouri: Columbia, 1991: 53-63.
Dean, Andrea Oppenheimer. "Their Own" [on Andres Duany and Elizabeth Plater-Zyberk's community planning]. *Historic Preservation* 44.3 (May/June 1992): 56-61.
Dietz, Paula. "Sitting in the Garden." *The Magazine Antiques* CXLI.6 (June 1992): 978-989.
Downing, A.J. *The Architecture of Country Houses*. 1850. New York: DaCapo, 1968.
_____. *Rural Essays*. New York: Leavitt and Allen, 1855.
_____. *A Treatise on the Theory and Practice of Landscape Gardening*. Boston: Wiley & Putnam, 1841.
Druse, Ken. *The Natural Garden*. New York: Clarkson Potter, 1988.
Dwight, H.G. "Gardens and Gardens." *Atlantic* July 1912: 61-68.
Earle, Alice Morse. *Old Time Gardens. A Book of the Sweet O' The Year*. New York: Macmillan, 1927.
Eberlein, Harold Donaldson, and Cortlandt van Dyke Hubbard. *The Practical Book of Garden Structure and Design*. Philadelphia: Lippincott, 1937.
"Eclipse of the Family Porch." *American Mercury* 77 (Aug. 1953): 135-136.
Edwards, Arthur M. *The Design of Suburbia, A Critical Study in Environmental History*. London: Pembridge, 1981.
Fales, Winnifred, and Mary Northend. "The Outdoor Living Room." *The Independent* 4 May 1918: 205.
Flexner, James Thomas. *Nineteenth Century American Painting*. New York: G.P. Putnam's Sons, 1970.
Francis, Mark and Randolph T. Hester, Jr. *The Meaning of Gardens*. Cambridge: MIT P, 1990.
Gabelman, Fred. "Roadway and Lawn Space Widths and Maintenance in Kansas City, Missouri." *American City* Oct. 1912: 350-353.
Geyer, O.R. "Cleaning and Beautifying a City." *American City* 16.4 (Apr. 1917): 365-368.
Glaab, Charles A., and Morgan Barclay. *Toledo, Gateway to the Great Lakes*. Tulsa: Continental Heritage P, 1982.

Glassman, Michael. "A Front-Yard Makeover: Good Fences Make Good Neighbors." *Fine Gardening* Mar./Apr. 1989: 60-65.
"A Good Lawn." *Scientific American* 20 Feb. 1875: 118.
"Goodbye, Old Friend." *Collier's* 131 (16 May 1953): 74.
Gordon, Elizabeth. "A Garden is American Style...." *House Beautiful* Feb. 1951: 55-58, 152-158.
———. "Does Your Front Lawn Belong to You—*or the Whole Neighborhood? House Beautiful* May 1960: 152, 232-234.
Gothein, Marie Luise. *A History of Garden Art*. New York: Dutton, 1928.
Goffman, Erving. *The Presentation of Self in Everyday Life*. Garden City: Doubleday-Anchor, 1959.
Gowans, Alan. *The Comfortable House: North American Suburban Architecture 1890-1930.* Cambridge: MIT P, 1986.
Grampp, Christopher. "Gardens for California Living." *Landscape* 28.3 (1985): 40-47.
"Growth of Cities in the United States." *Harper's Monthly* July 1853: 171-175.
Haldeman, B. Antrim. "The Control of Municipal Development by the 'Zone System' and Its Application in the United States." *American City* Sept. 1912: 222-225.
Hall, Edward T. *The Hidden Dimension*. New York: Doubleday, 1966.
Handlin, David P. *The American Home: Architecture and Society, 1815-1915*. Boston: Little, Brown, 1979.
Harper, Roland M. "Some Interesting Statistics of Fencing." Pub. G. Ward Hubbs in *Alabama Review* 37.3 (1984): 221-226.
Hayter, Earl W. "Livestock Fencing Conflicts in Rural America." *Agricultural History* 37:1 (1963): 10-20.
Henderson, Peter. *Gardening for Pleasure. A Guide to the Amateur in the Fruit, Vegetable, and Flower Garden, with full directions for the Greenhouse, Conservatory, and Window Garden*. New York: Orange Judd, 1883.
"Here is How to Handle a Useless Porch." *Better Homes & Gardens* 30 (Mar. 1952): 232-233.
Hill, Amelia Leavitt. *Redeeming Old Homes, Country Homes for Modest Purses*. New York: Holt, 1923.
Holly, Henry Hudson. *Holly's Country Seats*. New York: D. Appleton, 1866.

"Horace Engle's Candid Camera." *American Heritage* 16.2 (Feb. 1975): 4-11. Corner lot 1888-1889 Marietta, PA, 11.

Hoskins, W.G. *The Making of the English Landscape*. London: Penguin Books, 1955.

"House Hunting in Licking County." *American Heritage* 37.2 (Feb./Mar. 1986): 100-105. Comparative views of houses circa 1907 and 1982: 100, 103.

"How to Make a Garden—The Lawn." *Country Life in America* Mar. 1902: 173.

Howland, Joseph E. "The American Style Garden is Informal and Natural." *House Beautiful* Feb. 1951: 68-75.

_____. "Why has America Invented Its Own Style in Gardens?" *House Beautiful* Feb. 1951: 76-78.

"A Hundred Years from the Scythe." *Garden Magazine* 37 (June 1923): 268-269. Ills. Of 11 hand and power mowers circa 1830-1923.

Illustrated Historical Atlas of Lucas and Part of Wood Counties Ohio. Andreas & Baskin: Chicago, 1875.

"An Improved Lawn Mower." *Scientific American* (5 Apr. 1879): 211.

Jackson, J.B. "Urban Circumstances," *Design Quarterly* 128 (1985).

Jackson, John Brinckerhoff. *American Space: The Centennial Years 1865-1876*. Norton: New York 1972.

Jacob, Kathryn Allamong. "She Couldn't Have Done It Even If She Did." *American Heritage* 19.2 (Feb./Mar. 1978): 42-53. Photo of Borden home 1893, 48.

Jacob, Preminda. "A Dialectic of Personal and Communal Aesthetics: Paradigms of Yard Ornamentation in Northeastern America." *Journal of Popular Culture* 26.3 (Winter 1992): 91-105.

Jakle, John A. *The American Small Town: Twentieth-Century Place Images*. Hamden: Archon, 1982.

James, C.H., and F.R. Yerbury. *Small Houses for the Community*. London: Crosby Lockwood, 1928.

James, Harlean. "Civic Gardening, Which Develops the City People." *The Craftsman* 25 (Mar. 1914): 574-584.

Jeane, D. Gregory. "The Upland South Folk Cemetery Complex: Some Suggestion of Origin." *Cemeteries and Gravemarkers: Voices of America Culture*. Ed. Richard E. Meyer. Ann Arbor: UMI, 1989.

Johnson, Esther. "Back Yard Versus Front Porch." *House Beautiful* June 1922: 602-606.

Johnson, Paul C. *Farm Inventions in the Making of America*. Des Moines: Wallace-Homestead, 1976.

Jordan, Cora. *Neighbor Law: Fences, Trees, Boundaries & Noise*. Berkeley: Nolo P, 1991.

Kern, G.M. *Practical Landscape Gardening with Reference to the Improvement of Rural Residences*. Cincinnati: Moore, Wilstach, Keys, 1853.

Koegler, Karen. "Mulch and Taxus: The Suburban Front Yard Revisited." Paper presented at the Popular Culture Association national meeting, Apr. 1992.

Kostof, Spiro. *America By Design*. Oxford UP: New York, 1987.

Kouwenhoven, John A. *The Columbia Historical Portrait of New York*. Garden City: Doubleday, 1953.

Kubler, George. *The Shape of Time: Remarks of the History of Things*. New Haven: Yale, 1962.

"Lawn Mowers." Anonymous broadside published by Julius Bien & Co., Photolith New York 1884? Illustrates nine lawn mowers date 1830-1884. *Verso* has 12 agricultural mowers 1799-1884.

"Lawn Mowing Made a Pleasure." *Scientific American* 4 Sept. 1880: 146.

"Lawns—How to Make and Keep Them." *Scientific American* 1 Apr. 1876: 210.

Leccese, Michael. "Berm: A Four Letter Word." *Landscape Architecture* 82.4 (Apr. 1992): 69-70.

Leighton, Ann. *American Gardens of the Nineteenth Century For Comfort and Affluence*. Amherst: U of Massachusetts, 1987.

Lewis, Peirce. "Axioms for Reading the Landscape; Some Guides to the American Scene." *The Interpretation of Ordinary Landscapes*. Ed. D.W. Meinig. New York: Oxford UP, 1979: 11-32.

Licht, Avis Rappoport. "A Welcoming Entry, Redesigning a Small Front Yard." *Fine Gardening* 19 (May/June 1991): 26-29.

Longstreth, Richard, ed. *The Mall in Washington, 1791-1991*. Studies in the History of Art 30, National Gallery of Art; Washington, 1991.

Loudon, J.C. *An Encyclopedia of Gardening; Comprising the Theory and Practice of Horticulture, Floriculture, Arboriculture, and Landscape Gardening; Including all the Latest Improvements, a General History of Gardening in all Countries; and a Statistical View of Its Present State; with Suggestions for Its Future Progress in the British Isles*. A New Edition, Corrected and Improved by Mrs. London. Longman, Brown, Green, and Longmans: London, 1850.

Lowen, Sara. "The Tyranny of the Lawn." *American Heritage* 42.5 (Sept. 1991): 44-55.

Maciejak, Dan. "Back to Meadows." *Old-House Journal* Mar. 1981: 59-60.

March, Ada. "Fences in Towns and Villages." *American Homes & Gardens* 5 (Mar. 1908): 93.

Maxwell, Mary Mortimer. "The Lack of Privacy in the American Home." *Living Age* 269 (20 May 1911): 451-456.

McGuire, Diane Kostial. *Gardens of America, Three Centuries of Design.* Charlottesville, VA: Thomasson-Grant, 1989.

Meier, Lauren and Betsy Chittenden. *Preserving Historic Landscapes: An Annotated Bibliography.* National Park Service Preservation Assistance Division: Washington D.C., 1990.

"Merging City Backyards." *Commonweal* 50 (10 June 1949): 212.

"Metal Fences for Tenement Yards." *American City* Mar. 1917: 262-263.

Miller, Wilhelm. *The Prairie Spirit in Landscape Gardening* Circular 184, Illinois Agricultural Experimental Station: Urbana, Nov. 1915.

_____. *The Illinois Way of Beautifying the Farm.* Circular 170, U of Illinois Agricultural Experiment Station: Urbana, 1914.

"Monta-Mower—Two Advantages, Two Shortcomings." *Consumer Reports* July 1948: 307.

Moore, Chris D. "A Front-Yard Retreat." *Fine Gardening* 26 (July-Aug. 1992): 30-33.

Morris, A.E.J. *History of Urban Form Before the Industrial Revolutions.* New York: John Wiley & Sons, 1979.

"A Motor Lawn Mower." *Scientific American* 13 Nov. 1897: 314.

"Mowers" (36 models of push reel-mowers). *Consumer Reports* July 1949: 306-10.

Murray, Pauline. *Planning and Planting the Home Garden.* New York: Orange Judd, 1932.

Nabokov, Peter, and Robert Easton. *Native American Architecture.* New York: Oxford UP, 1989.

"New York Yards." *American Architect and Building News* 5 (1879): 163-164, Part II, 173-174.

Newton, Norman T. *Design on the Land: The Development of Landscape Architecture.* Cambridge: Harvard, 1971.

Noble, Allen G. *Wood, Brick and Stone: The North American Settlement Pattern.* Vol 2. Amherst: U of Massachusetts, 1984.

Olmart, Michael. "Points of Origin." *Smithsonian* June 1984: 36, 38.

Olmsted, Frederick Law. "Village Improvement." *Atlantic* 95 (June 1905): 798-803.

_____. "Riverside, Illinois, A Residential Neighbor-Hood Designed Over Sixty Years Ago." (Selections from the Papers of Frederick Law Olmsted, Senior) *Landscape Architecture* XXI: 4 (July 1931).

"On Our Fenceless State."*Atlantic* Aug. 1909: 283-284.

Orlando, Richard. "Lawn Logic, An Intelligent Approach to Grass." *Horticulture* XVIII.5 (May 1990): 20-25.

Parrington, V.L. "On The Lack of Privacy in American Village Homes." *House Beautiful* 13.2 (Jan. 1903): 109-112.

"Passing of the Old Front Porch." ("the Contributors' Club"), *House & Garden* 101 (June 1952): 68f.

Peter Henderson & Co. Catalog of *Seeds and Lawn and Garden Requisites*. New York, 1988.

Peterson, Fred. "Philadelphia Lawn Mower." *Scientific American* 20 Apr. 1878: 249.

Peterson, Fred W. *Homes in the Heartland: Balloon Frame Farmhouses of the Upper Midwest, 1850-1920*. Lawrence KS: UP of Kansas, 1992.

Philadelphia Lawn Mowers for 1872. Catalog by Robert Buist Junior for Graham, Emlen & Passmore.

Pollan, Michael. *Second Nature, A Gardeners Education*. New York: Atlantic Monthly P, 1991.

Pope, Alexandar. "An Essay on Criticism." 1711. Line 89.

Post, Emily. *The Personality of a House, The Blue Book of Home Charm*. 1930. New York: Funk & Wagnalls, 1948.

Powell, E.P. *Hedges, Windbreaks, Shelters and Live Fences*. New York: Orange Judd, 1910.

"Power Lawn Mowers." *Consumer Research Bulletin* Aug. 1950: 9-12.

"Power Mowers." *Consumer Reports* 1948 Buying Guide June: 254-259, July: 309, Sept.: 406-407.

Renaud, Wayne, and Gordon Webber. "Welcoming Waters. A Front Yard Pool Makes a Soothing Entry." *Fine Gardens* 25 (May/June 1992): 30-33.

Reps, John W. *Views and Viewmakers of Urban America. Lithographs of Towns and Cities in the United States and Canada, Notes on the Artists and Publishers, and a Union Catalog of Their Work 1825-1925*. Columbia: U of Missouri P, 1984.

Riverside: A Village in a Park. Riverside, IL: The Frederick Law Olmsted Society of Riverside, 1970.

Rogers, Everett M. *Diffusion of Innovations*. New York: Free, 1962.
Samuelson, Robert J. "The Joys of Mowing." *Newsweek* 29 Apr. 1991: 49.
Schroeder, Fred E.H. "The Democratic Yard and Garden." *Outlaw Aesthetics: Arts and the Public Mind*. Bowling Green, OH: Bowling Green State University Popular Press, 1977.
_____. "Schoolhouse Reading; What You Can Learn from Your Rural School." *History News* 36.4 (Apr. 1981): 15-16.
Scott, Frank J. *The Art of Beautifying Suburban Home Grounds*, etc., D. Appleton: New York, 1870. (Facsimile edition by American Life Foundation). Also 1886 edition by John B. Alden: New York.
[Scott] "An Inventory of the Jesup W. and Frank J. Scott Papers in the Toledo-Lucas County Public Library." 2 July 1975.
Scott, Frank Jesup. "Autobiography." Manuscript in Scott papers, Local History Department Toledo-Lucas County Public Library.
Scott Papers. Transcription from Toledo *Daily Blade* 7 Aug. 1905: 5.
"Set-Back Lines as an Aid to Better and Cheaper Street Layouts." *American City* 16.2 (Feb. 1917): 144-148.
"Short History of the Lawn Mower Industry." See *Coldwell Lawn Mowers*.
Sloan's Homestead Architecture Containing Forty Designs for Villas, Cottages and Farm Houses with Essays on Style, Construction, Landscape Gardening, Furniture, Etc. Etc. Philadelphia: Lippincott, 1861.
"Small Bright World of Anna Lindner." *American Heritage* 27.1 (Dec. 1975): 4-10. Views of house and grounds circa 1895, 5-6.
"Smaller Spaces: Six Success Stories." *Garden Design* 8:3 (Autumn 1989): 25-57.
Smith, Edith Dunham. "How I Did It; Porches, Past and Present: The Story of a Transformation." *House Beautiful* (Apr. 1925): 402.
Smith, Suzanne. "An American Panorama." *American Heritage* 26: 3 (Apr. 1974): 44-53. Snapshots of Corning NY 1899-1900. 52-53 street scene.
Solving Landscape Problems. (Better Homes & Gardens Home Video). Des Moines: Meredith, 1989.
Sprague, Paul E. *Guide to Frank Lloyd Wright & Prairie School Architecture in Oak Park*. Oak Park, IL, 1986.
Stilgoe, John R. *Borderland: Origins of the America Suburb 1820-1939*. New Haven: Yale UP, 1988.

_____. *Common Landscape in America, 1580-1845*. New Haven: Yale UP, 1982

_____. "The Suburbs." *American Heritage* 35.2 (Feb., Mar. 1984): 20-37.

Strawn, John. *Driving the Green: The Making of a Golf Course*. New York: Harper Collins, 1991.

The Swan. Prod. Dore Schary for MGM (1956). Has scene of servant scything a palace lawn.

Taft, Robert. *Photography and the American Scene*. New York: Macmillan, 1938. Yards in every early photograph 116, 284, 291, 429, 432.

Thaxter, Celia. *An Island Garden* (with pictures and illuminations by Childe Hassam). 1894. Boston: Houghton Mifflin, 1988.

Thoreau, Henry David. *Walden or Life in the Woods*, New York: Heritage, 1939.

Tice, Patricia M. *Gardening in America 1830-1910*. Rochester: Strong Museum, 1984.

_____. "Garden of Change." *American Home Life, 1880-1930*. Eds. Jessica Foy and Thomas Schlereth. Knoxville: U of Tennessee P, 1992: 190-208.

Toledo City Directory, 1877-1878.

Toledo Illustrated. New York: International Publishing Co., 1888.

Townsend, Gavin. "Airborne Toxins and the American House 1865-1895." *Winterthur Portfolio* 24.1 (Spring 1989): 29-42.

Tunnard, Christopher, and Henry Hope Reed. *American Skyline: The Growth and Form of Our Cities and Towns*. New York: New American Library, 1956.

Upton, Dell. "Outside the Academy: A Century of Vernacular Architecture Studies, 1890-1990." *Studies in the History of Art 33* (1990): 199-213.

Waggoner, Clark, ed. *History of Toledo and Lucas County, Ohio*. 2 vols. New York and Toledo: Mansell & Co., 1888.

Ward, Daniel Franklin, ed. *Personal Places; Perspectives on Informal Art Environments*. Bowling Green, OH: Bowling Green State University Popular Press, 1984.

Ward, Geoffrey C. *Lincoln and His Family*. Springfield: Sangamon State U, 1978. View of Lincoln home in 1860: 18-19.

Watts, May Thielgaard. *Reading the Landscape: An Adventure in Ecology*. New York: Macmillan, 1957.

Watts, May Thielgaard, and Frederick McGourty. "The Stylish House-Revisited." *Flower and Garden* Aug.-Sept. 1988: 34-39.

Waugh, F.A. *Landscape Gardening. A Treatise on the General Principles Governing Outdoor Art; With Sundry Suggestions for Their Application in the Commoner Problems of Gardening,* 1899.

"We Miss Our Front Porch." *American Home* 47 (Apr. 1952): 47.

Westmacott, Richard. *African-American Gardens and Yards in the Rural South.* Knoxville: U of Tennessee P, 1992.

"What Can You Do With A Front Porch." *Better Homes & Gardens* 29 (June 1951): 150.

"What Does Your *Neighbor* See?" *Good Housekeeping* July 1940: 142.

White, Christie. "Documenting and Interpreting Early 19th Century Rural Gardens at Old Stubridge Village." Proceedings of the 1989 Annual Meeting (of ALHFAM), XII: 1992, Association for Living Historical Farms and Agricultural Museums: Sante Fe, 1992: 189-195.

Williams, Ottalie K. "Your Grounds Are *Everybody s* Business." *American Home* Apr. 1948: 22.

Wolkomir, Richard. "Mownomaniacs Take the Sword to the Sward." *Smithsonian* May 1990: 166.

Wright, Frank Lloyd. "A Home in a Prairie Town." *Ladies Home Journal* XVIII: 3 (Feb. 1901): 17.